About the Authors

Joan D. Johnson is Professor of Physical Education, former women's tennis coach and former Chair of the Department of Physical Education and Athletics at California State University, Los Angeles. She has attended Western Michigan University in Kalamazoo and she received her B.S. degree from the University of Wisconsin. She also attended the University of Michigan and earned the M.S. in Education and Ph.D. degrees at the University of Southern California. She is an experienced tournament competitor and has competed in three of the four Grand Slam events—the championships of Australia, England (Wimbledon) and the United States—while traveling extensively for both competitive and educational purposes. She has been selected as United States Women's Tennis Coach for the World University Games and for USTA Junior Wightman Cup teams. In addition, Dr. Johnson has directed many tennis coaching clinics and workshops. She served for many years as a member of the USTA Women's Collegiate Committee, as Chair of the Large College Tennis Committee of the Association for Intercollegiate Athletics for Women and as a member of the Southern California Tennis Umpires Association. She was director for the AIAW Division II National Tennis Championship and she continues to serve on tournament committees.

Dr. Johnson is coauthor of *A Workbook for Tests and Measurements in Physical Education* (with David Kelley) and has held many elective and appointive offices in several professional organizations, including Western Society for Physical Education of College Women, California Association for Health, Physical Education, Recreation and Dance and the American Alliance for Health, Physical Education, Recreation and Dance.

Paul J. Xanthos is professor of Health, Physical Education, and Recreation, and former Chair of the Department of Health, Physical Education, and Recreation for men at Los Angeles Pierce College in Woodland Hills, California. He earned the A.B. degree at Occidental College and the M.S. degree, General Secondary and General Administrative Credentials at the University of Southern California. As an undergraduate student-athlete at Occidental, he participated in intercollegiate track and field in addition to leading, and in his last year, coaching the tennis team.

Professor Xanthos has authored *Tennis—A Pictorial Guide for Teachers, Handbook for Tennis Class Organization,* and *Handbook for Conduct and Organization of Tennis Clinics and Teacher Training Workshops* as well as numerous articles for professional magazines and journals. Recently, he wrote the chapter on basic skills for the SEIKO and USPTA publication—*Tennis: A*

Professional Guide. His film, "Tennis, Sport of a Lifetime on Tennis Class Organization" is considered a classic in group instruction.

As tennis coach at North Hollywood High School, Xanthos' tennis teams compiled an amazing 128–7 league record with 14 championships and four second places in 18 years. As varsity coach at Los Angeles Pierce College, he has led his teams to 4 consecutive Western State Conference Championships and thirteen Metropolitan Conference Championships, ten consecutive since 1976 (241 wins—96 consecutive; 20 losses). He was selected "Conference Coach of the Year" 17 times and in April 1987 was honored as "Outstanding Educator" at the Pierce College Foundation Annual Awards Banquet. In 1979, he was selected by the California Coaches Association as the "California Community College Coach of the Year," and in 1984, was the first recipient of the Wilson Sporting Goods Company Award of "California Community College Tennis Coach of the Year." In 1984, Xanthos also received the California Division United States Professional Tennis Association Coach of the Year Award and the USPTA National Coach of the Year Award. He was also named a USPTA Master Professional.

In 1974, Xanthos was corecipient (with Vic Braden) of the National Tennis Foundation (USLTA) Award of Merit for his "contributions to the development of tennis in the United States." He has conducted over 400 tennis teachers' clinics and workshops throughout the world and is recognized as one of the world's leading exponents of large group instruction.

Professor Xanthos was honored by the United States Professional Tennis Association with an honorary membership and is currently a regular member and officer of the USPTA; he also serves as a regional tester for prospective members. He is a staff member of the Lifetime Sports Education Project, a charter member of the USTA Education and Research Committee, and State Chair of the CAHPERD All Golf Clinic and Tennis Workshop.

2201

TENNIS

WM. C. BROWN SPORTS AND FITNESS SERIES

TENNIS

Joan D. Johnson
California State University, Los Angeles

Paul J. Xanthos
Los Angeles Pierce College

Fifth Edition

wcb
Wm. C. Brown Publishers
Dubuque, Iowa

Consulting Editors

Physical Education
Aileene Lockhart
Texas Woman's University

Parks and Recreation
David Gray
California State University, Long Beach

Health
Robert Kaplan
The Ohio State University

WCB Sports and Fitness Series
Evaluation Materials Editor
Jane A. Mott
Texas Woman's University

Cover photograph © David Madison 1987

Library of Congress Catalog Card Number: 87–70262

ISBN 0–697–00363–9

Printed in the United States of America
10 9 8 7 6 5 4 3 2 1

Contents

Preface

This book is written for the student of tennis. While the basic material is presented in a style easily comprehensible to the beginner, the depth of the material, when thoroughly mastered, should lead to intermediate and advanced levels of knowledge and skill.

The book presents basic descriptions of tennis skills, some of the underlying reasons which support the descriptions, a condensation and interpretation of the rules as well as the unwritten rules, and a discussion of strategy which should be helpful both to the player who wishes to develop a personalized pattern of play and to the spectator who wishes to become more aware of what is really happening while watching others play. Other chapters deal with the selection and care of equipment, with tennis organizations, and with suggestions for playing the game.

Response to earlier editions has been most gratifying; and we are indebted to our critics and reviewers who have made several helpful suggestions, many of which are incorporated in this extensively revised fifth edition.

The first chapter provides a brief overview of the game; many readers will already be familiar with some of this material, but before proceeding, each reader is encouraged to study the name of each line on the court and in addition, to become acquainted with the names of the parts of the racket. If this information has been learned well, you will be able to follow subsequent instructions and descriptions much more easily.

Chapters Two and Three contain revised stroke descriptions, a new comparative analysis of the forehand and backhand drives which serves as a checklist of reminders for each stroke; a new section on footwork with clear illustrations of each pattern; clearly defined photographs and sections on the two-handed backhand, the return of serve and approaching the net.

Chapter Four provides advice on conditioning, warm-up, and suggested practice drills, plus a thorough description of the graduated length method for learning groundstrokes, serve, and volley.

The presentation of strategy in Chapter Five is one of the most thorough available in a book of this size and many diagrams are included to clarify and illustrate the points presented.

Over a period of many years the rules of tennis had not changed, but in the last several years, suddenly there have been quite a few rule changes. Thus, Chapter Six includes references to the new rule numbers and has been updated. Descriptions of no-ad scoring and the twelve-point tiebreaker are also included, along with new diagrams illustrating tiebreaker procedures for both singles and doubles.

Chapter Seven on the unwritten rules has not changed substantively, but appropriate headings enhance readability and facilitate the location of material related to specific situations. In the previous edition, we included a new self-evaluating quiz titled "Do You Know the Score?" with questions and situations appropriate for persons of all skill levels, and especially for those who may be venturing forth into their first competitive experiences. This has been very favorably received as a most helpful mechanism for developing true understanding of tennis etiquette as well as thoughtful, sportsmanlike behavior. (See Appendix 2.)

Throughout the years, tennis players have developed a wide variety of techniques and styles of play—all designed to outmaneuver the opponent and win the point. That such variety of method exists for the purpose of obtaining but a single objective is silent testimony to the resourcefulness of those who play. Tennis has a rich and fascinating history, not only with respect to its past and its continuing development, but also with respect to the interesting personalities who have influenced this development. A thorough study of this aspect of the game would require several volumes and thus is beyond the scope of this publication, but parts of the story are told in the following pages, especially in Chapter Eight, which contains definitions of the colorful terminology of tennis.

Chapters Nine and Ten have been updated to incorporate the wealth of options now available in selecting equipment, the changes in USTA membership categories, the addition of the National Tennis Rating Program, a section on increasing opportunities for the spectator, and things to look for while you are watching, besides many other fascinating facts for the tennis enthusiast. An updated selected reference list follows Chapter Ten and will help the reader to personally discover the tennis story.

We think you will enjoy this new edition and hope that you will find the information to help you move through the ranks from beginner to intermediate to advanced and beyond! Self-evaluation questions pertaining to both knowledge and skill are distributed throughout the text. These afford the reader examples of the kinds of understanding and levels of skill that should be acquired as progress is made toward mastery of tennis. Try to respond to these questions thoroughly and competently, and devise additional ones to further stimulate your learning. You may find that you cannot respond fully and accurately to a question until you have read more extensively or gained more playing experience. From time to time, return to such troublesome questions until you are sure of the answers or have developed the required skills. Answers to the self-evaluation questions may be found on p. 145.

The knowledge test, included for both student and instructor use, is organized into eight units, providing 15 to 20 questions for each topic. Both the test items and the answers are provided in Appendix 1.

The authors wish to extend their appreciation to Sue Powell and Jeri Shepard for the illustrations and to Mary Pat Faley, Alejandra Ordonez, Paul Steele, Yvette Bettar, Bob Collins, Peter Holliday, and Doreen Irish, the models in the photographs.

1 What Tennis Is Like

Tennis is played around the world under the same rules and scoring system: in schools and colleges, on private courts, in public parks, in exclusive clubs, in big cities and small towns, and both indoors and outdoors. It is played on a court 78 feet long and 36 feet wide divided by a tautly strung net three and a half feet high at the posts but only 3 feet high in the center (fig. 1.1). Singles is played by two players opposing each other on a narrower court (27′ wide); when four players play, two on one side opposing two on the other, the full court (36′ wide) is used and the game is called doubles. Each player uses a racket made of ceramic fibers, wood, aluminum, fiberglass, graphite, carbon or combinations thereof, strung with synthetic materials or gut, to hit a rubber, felt-covered ball back and forth across the net, within the boundaries of the court.

Rules of the game impose some highly specific conditions upon the players, but the general idea is to hit the ball into your opponent's court in such a way that your opponent is unable to return it to your court or that the ball is returned

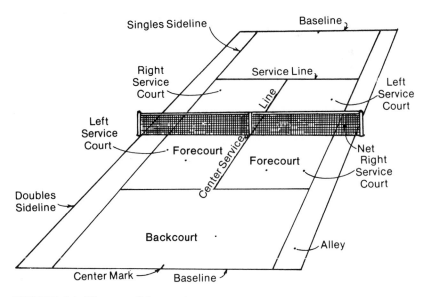

FIGURE 1.1 Diagram of the court

so weakly that you can surely "put it away" with your next shot. This may sound as though points are decided by one or two shots; while this does happen in contests between "big game" stylists, usually it takes many more shots to maneuver your opponent out of position, especially when the opponent is trying to do the same thing to you.

The game is started when one player, standing behind the baseline to the right of the center mark, tosses the ball up and serves to the opponent. The serve must go over the net and must land in the diagonally opposite right service court. If the first serve is unsuccessful, the server has another chance. If that, too, is a fault, the receiver wins the point. The second point is started from the left of the center mark and the serve is directed to the left service court. The third point is started as the first, in the right court, and so on until the game is over. If a serve is good, the receiver attempts to return the ball anywhere into the opponent's court. The rally continues until one player hits the ball into the net or outside the opponent's court boundaries or lets the ball bounce twice before returning it, in which case, the point is lost. The served ball *must bounce* in the proper service court, but after the serve, a player may elect to move in toward the net to hit the ball before it bounces and make a shot called a volley. If one player has advanced to the net, the opponent may try to lob the ball over the head of the net player; if the lob is too short to be truly effective, the net player may be able to reach up and smash it back into the opponent's court. At the end of the first game, the server becomes the receiver and vice versa; players alternate thus throughout the match. A player must win at least four points to win a game, at least six games to win a set, and at least two sets to win a match.

Similarities between the skills of tennis and the skills of other games will be noticed by the discerning reader. For example, the ready position and footwork in tennis is often compared with that of basketball. The tennis two-step may also be found on a dance floor. The sidearm movement pattern used to hit most groundstrokes is similar to that used by the baseball batter. The overhead swing of the tennis serve and smash contains many of the same elements as the badminton clear and smash, the overhand pitch in baseball, and the volleyball overhand serve. Volleying in tennis has been likened to the boxer's jab and to the reaching movement used to catch a ball out in front. Other comparisons could be made, but these will be left to the reader.

VALUES

All kinds of people play tennis, and they play for many reasons. Tennis can truly be called the sport of a lifetime, since youngsters can begin at about six years of age and their grandparents may still be playing even past age seventy! Young and old, men and women, highly skilled champions and eager beginners all express their enthusiasm for the game both on and off the court. Execution of the strokes demands coordination and skill, fine timing of racket, arm, body, and feet. Stamina and endurance are required to persist through long rallies and matches, but healthy exercise is provided for all, even at the moderate pace of intermediate players. The challenge of outwitting the opponent exists at all levels of skill, and many a match has been won by the less skilled player through the application of superior tactics. Understanding one's strengths in order to exploit the opponent's weaknesses demands keen analysis and quick anticipation. It requires self-discipline to practice purposefully and self-control to persist throughout the sometimes trying conditions of match play. Raising one's game to meet the demands of competition can produce a most satisfying feeling. Finally, tennis provides a marvelous social situation. Only one other person is necessary to play, but many people all over the world *do* play, and the friendly spirit inherent in the words, "Would you like to hit some?" or, as the English say, "Let's have a knock, shall we?" is all the introduction you need. Issue this invitation yourself, and you'll soon see what fun it is!

COURTS

Courts come in a variety of surfaces and surroundings. While the official rules specify the dimensions of the court, the height and location of the net posts, the width of the lines, and the like, nothing is said about the court surface. Grass, clay, concrete, asphalt, wood, composition, and several other types of surfaces are currently used. The USTA lists approximately 100 brands of court surfaces, and as the popular interest in tennis continues to grow, so does the list. The major categories of court surfaces follow.

1. Grass was the original surface for "lawn tennis"; in the early days people would string nets on the lawns of their estates or carry their own nets to the lawns of the local parks. A field of grass courts provides a lush and colorful setting and a surface that is easy on the feet. The ball tends to skid into a low trajectory and may bounce inconsistently and unpredictably as a result of irregularities in the turf, thus encouraging an aggressive style of play in which players hit the ball before it bounces (volley) and move in to control the net. Grass courts demand continuous and costly maintenance procedures and are no longer the predominant court surface. Only two of the world's major championships, the Australian and the All-England (Wimbledon), are still played on grass.
2. Clay-type courts, sometimes called soft courts, are those with a loose, granular surface which is easy on the feet and permits players to slide into their shots. The ball bounce is high, thus producing a slower game in which players have more time to retrieve opponents' shots and to get set to hit their own returns. Emphasis is on steadiness and consistency from the backcourt because it is difficult to put the ball away on the slow surface. Even though extensive maintenance procedures are required, this is the most common surface throughout the world and many major championships are played on clay.
3. Hard courts are those made of concrete, asphalt, wood or composition materials and, as the name implies, the surface is hard on the feet and legs. The surface produces a consistent, medium-high bounce, although the speed of the bounce can vary considerably depending on the degree of roughness left in the finished surface (the smoother the surface, the faster and lower the bounce). These courts provide secure footing for quick starts and stops. Most courts are colored (usually green inside the lines and red outside) to reduce

glare and facilitate ball visibility. Some composition courts add a resilient layer of material to a concrete or asphalt base which provides a comfortable sponginess underfoot and produces a slightly higher, slower bounce. Installation costs vary considerably but, once installed, maintenance procedures are relatively easy and inexpensive. Hard courts are the predominant surface in the United States.

4. Synthetic and artificial surfaces will most likely be seen while you are watching the pros play in an indoor arena. These textile and plastic carpets can be placed on top of almost any surface, usually a hard surface, and they provide a certain degree of consistency for the players as they compete at various sites around the world.

Most tennis experts agree that the surface influences, to a considerable degree, the type of rebound and thus the effectiveness of various strokes, strategies, and styles of play. A beginner could probably care less about the court surface, but as you gain in skill and experience, and venture forth to a variety of playing sites, the game of tennis will become more enjoyable if you are aware of the differences in court surfaces. Take the time to adjust your timing and footwork to the bounce of the ball and the speed of the play. Whatever the surface, before you play, see that the court is safe. Remove loose dirt, leaves, glass, or other objects on which you might slip or fall, and close the gates to prevent running into one unexpectedly left open. (This also prevents much unnecessary ball chasing.)

DRESS

Significant improvements have been made in the design and construction of tennis shoes. Support, comfort, flexibility, durability, style, weight, size and cost are criteria most commonly applied to shoe selection. Effective footwear is necessary for quick starts and stops, for running up, back, and side to side, for the lunges of volleys and the jumps of smashes demanded by the game of tennis. Selecting the right shoe for your type of foot, the court surface on which the shoe will usually be worn, and your style of play from the hundreds of shoes currently available is a difficult but important task.

Uppers are commonly made from canvas, leather, nylon mesh, polypropylene or a combination of these materials. Nylon mesh or polypropylene, which are lighter and provide better evaporation of perspiration thus cooler feet, in combination with leather, which reinforces areas of stress thus providing durability and increased support, is becoming an increasingly popular choice. Other features to consider include: rigid plastic inserts to stabilize the support provided by conventional heel counters; a midsole wedge for increased cushioning and for lifting the heel slightly to facilitate an on-your-toes quick start; removable and cushioned insoles which can be molded to the shape of your foot; and outer soles made of dual and multidensity natural and/or synthetic rubber, polyurethane, EVA (ethylene vinyl acetate), and combinations of these materials.

Two pairs of socks, the inner pair of cotton and the outer pair of wool, help to prevent blisters and also help to cushion the shock of sudden starts and stops, especially when worn inside tennis shoes that fit well. A proper fit in socks is important; a size too large is no better than one too small.

Fashionable colored tennis apparel is becoming increasingly popular and more readily available. The traditional white tennis attire reflects heat better than other colors, especially bright or dark colors, so white is the best color to wear on a hot sunny day. It is most important to wear clothing that is comfortable and provides for the freedom of movement demanded by the game. Top tournament players are extremely conscious of their appearance. They wear clean, well-pressed, attractive clothing and present a neat, well-groomed appearance on the court. You too can appear on the court looking like a tennis player; this will help you to become a better one!

Generally, men wear knit shirts with collars and shorts made of cotton and polyester. Women wear a feminine version of the knit shirt either with shorts or with tennis skirts. Modern, drip-dry, nonwrinkle fabrics have greatly simplified caring for tennis clothing. Polypropylene, a sportswear fabric that "wicks" perspiration off your body rather than absorbing it, is a recent addition to the materials used in tennis clothing. Even though such fabrics increase the cost of the garment, the comfort, durability and ease of care make this type of shorts and skirts highly desirable. Many women wear tennis dresses made of various materials, and potential Wimbledon champions may have dresses designed especially for them by leading tennis fashion designers. Some design and sew their own dresses, making them plain or frilly to suit individual tastes. The keynotes in all designs, however, are comfort, freedom of action, and ease of care.

Some players wear wristbands or wristlets made of an absorbent, slightly elasticized material which helps to keep perspiration from the hands. All players should have some type of sweater or jacket to put on after playing to prevent too rapid cooling off or stiffening muscles. The choice of material and weight of the sweater or jacket depends upon playing conditions (for example, the amount of wind, the temperature, general weather), and although white is still a popular color, other colors are acceptable and are frequently used. In addition, caps, assorted styles of floppy hats, sunshades, headbands, towels, and other gear are used by individual players for a variety of reasons. However, you do not need to spend all your money on apparel; you will look good in inexpensive tennis clothing, provided it is clean and neat.

BALLS

The official United States Tennis Association rules provide a complete, detailed description of an acceptable tennis ball, and they specify the exact manner in which certain tests must be made. The ordinary player needs to know only that most balls are made of molded rubber, covered with a fuzzy wool felt or nylon material, and filled with pressurized air. Some balls are made without the compressed air center and achieve resilience from their rubber centers. Players may choose from a variety of colors, including white, orange, fuschia, optic yellow, and a combination of orange and yellow. Optic yellow seems to be the most popular among the better players, and many claim that the brighter colors enhance their ability to see the ball sooner. In official competition, the ball must be white or yellow in color (Rule 3).

Beginners, trying to economize on balls, frequently practice with used balls that have become light as a result of wearing down the material cover until only the skin is left. Skinned balls are impossible to control effectively, so that practicing with them may induce poor stroke habits. Give the skinless wonders to the dog, and give yourself a chance to start on the right track toward a lifetime of enjoyable tennis.

RACKETS

For many years, there was nothing in the rules about the racket; almost all rackets were made of wood and were relatively uniform in size (27″ long and 9″ wide across the face). Increasing interest and participation in tennis has motivated equipment manufacturers to experiment with new materials, new designs, different sizes, various weights, and creative stringing patterns. Some of these experiments produced rackets which changed the character of the game and eventually racket specifications were incorporated into the official rules. The major provisions of Rule 4 require that the hitting surface of the racket must be flat and that a pattern of crossed strings be generally uniform and connected to a frame. The frame shall not be longer than 32 inches nor wider than 12½ inches; the strung surface shall not be longer than 15½ inches nor wider than 11½ inches. Figure 1.2 shows five types of legal rackets. The important parts of the racket are labeled. More about the selection and care of equipment is presented in Chapter 9. For now, on with the game! Look again at figure 1.2 and figure 1.3. You should be able to identify the various parts of the racket so that the descriptions of the basic strokes in the next chapter will be as clear as possible.

FIGURE 1.2 Various types of rackets. From left to right, Wilson graphite, Prince ceramic, Prince magnesium, Adidas composite, and Prince Jr. Parts of the racket are labeled.

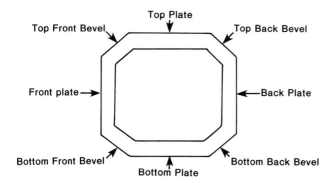

FIGURE 1.3 Butt of the racket

2 Skills Essential for Everyone

Before children can walk, they must learn to crawl, and before they can run, they must learn to walk. Before a player is able to employ the serve, the volley, the groundstrokes, the power, and the control of the "big game" of a champion, the newcomer must begin at the beginning and establish a sound foundation for future play. Bjorn Borg, Martina Navratilova, Boris Becker, Chris Evert Lloyd, John McEnroe, Ivan Lendl, Pam Shriver, Billie Jean King and other champions did not walk onto the tournament court without first spending countless hours on the practice court. Follow their example. Learn to grip the racket properly for the variety of strokes you will be called upon to make. Learn the basic ready or waiting position from which you will initiate a number of groundstrokes and volleys. Learn the footwork that will quickly propel you to the best position from which to execute your return. And finally, learn to execute the serve and the return of serve, two of the most important, and most frequently neglected, strokes in tennis. Master the basics and you will be well on your way to enjoying a lifetime of tennis.

This chapter will provide a framework of sound tennis fundamentals. Keep in mind that within this framework there is a certain amount of flexibility, a certain "range of correctness." There is no "only way" to hold your racket, no well-defined way to take your racket back when initiating the groundstroke, no exact length of backswing, no perfect point of impact. A slight turn of the hand on the grip, a straight back or circular backswing, a shorter or longer backswing, meeting the ball a little sooner or later, may produce the desired results. You need only observe the world-class players to see that all of them definitely do not come from the same mold. Nevertheless, start with the directions as they are presented. If these do not produce the results you want, experiment a little but stay within reasonable limits.

There are countless ways to learn the basic skills of tennis. Many of them are based on the past experiences of the teacher, e.g., the teacher's personal introduction to the game, instruction under a special teacher or coach, or experience as a member of a team. Others are the result of attendance at workshops, seminars or clinics designed to expand knowledge of methods of instruction, progressions, individual and group psychology, practice drills and training methods. Instruction may begin with the volley because it is a relatively simple stroke to learn and will provide early success, building confidence. You may begin with the serve because it is the stroke that initiates each point and is considered by many to be the most important stroke in tennis. You may begin with the backhand, which, for some reason, seems to provide an element of uncertainty for many beginners or you may begin with the forehand, which seems easiest to learn for many.

This presentation will begin with the groundstrokes, the forehand and backhand drives; each stroke will be described separately, although experience has suggested that the groundstrokes will be learned most effectively if they are presented and practiced simultaneously. A comparison of the grip, backswing, forward swing, follow-through, and finish will be presented in a summary section to facilitate the learning of comfortable stroking from both sides.

The directions are presented for the right-handed player; left-handers will need to reverse them.

THE READY POSITION

Tennis, like most sports, finds one side on the offense and the other on the defense. The stance assumed by both players is one of readiness. It is the position from which the player is ready to move *quickly* forward, back, side to side, and diagonally forward and back. Moreover, it is a *dynamic,* not a static position, with the player constantly alert and prepared to move quickly in any direction. Whether the player is waiting for the serve, at the net or at the baseline, the stance is similar. Slight variations are made on an individual basis, often depending upon the abilities of the player and the opponent. The initial position in singles is approximately three feet behind the baseline, somewhere near the center of the court. This is the position to which you will return for *most* baseline shots. Consider the following points when assuming the ready position (fig. 2.1):

1. Be ready for action. Face your opponent, feet comfortably spread (a little more than shoulder-width apart), knees bent (locked knees must be unlocked before quick movement can take place), body relaxed and weight slightly forward on the balls of the feet.

FIGURE 2.1 The basic ready position

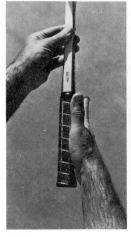

FIGURE 2.2 The forehand grip

2. Hold your racket in front of you about waist high, the throat resting (or cradled) on the fingers of your left hand, left thumb on top. Hold the racket handle loosely in the right hand with the forehand grip (fig. 2.2). Keep the head of the racket above the wrist, pointing slightly upward.
3. Point the head of your racket in the direction of your opponent, the end of the handle close enough to your body to make the position comfortable and without tension.

THE FOREHAND DRIVE

The forehand drive is used to contact a ball on the right side of a player's body. The stroker turns toward the right sideline with the left side pointing toward the net and with the forward foot, hip and shoulder directed toward the shot. As the ball is contacted, the palm of the hand, the wrist and the forearm move in the direction of the intended shot. The forehand is a fundamental stroke, and most players start their tennis play by hitting from the forehand side. Many feel it is the most important; therefore, it is essential to learn it properly from the beginning. The forehand drive, when properly executed, is a fluid, continuous motion; for ease and clarity of analysis, it is presented in its separate parts.

Grip

Several grips are used by the more advanced players and professionals, but most of these are only slight variations of the grip described here. This description will confine preliminary instruction to the Eastern forehand grip which will be referred to as the "forehand grip." As you advance, you may make slight adjustments and variations to suit your individual preferences. For the present, follow these instructions and refer to the photographs for clarification (figs. 1.3 and 2.2).

1. Rest the throat of your racket in the fingers of your left hand, thumb on top. The face of the racket is perpendicular to the ground, the racket head

"standing on edge," with the tip of the racket pointing to the net; the butt of the racket is in the center of, and a few inches away from, your body.

2. Place the palm of your hand against the back plate of the grip so that the palm and face of the racket are both on the same plane. Your hand is now in the "shake hands" position.

3. Close your hand and "shake hands with your racket." The grip must be firm enough for control but not too tight or rigid. *Spread the fingers,* making certain that the index finger is apart from the middle finger and is bent to form a "modified trigger finger."

4. Wrap your thumb around the grip until it touches the outside of your middle finger. The bottom of the base knuckle of your index finger is on the back plate of the grip. Looking down at the grip, you will see that the V formed by the thumb and index finger lines up with the center of the top plate or the top right edge of the grip.

5. This is your starting point. To allow for differences in the hand and racket handle, adjust your hand slightly so that the racket feels comfortable.

With this grip, the face of the racket becomes an extension of the palm of your hand, wrist and forearm. Holding the racket with this grip, turn your hand and wrist over and under, and note that the face of the racket makes similar changes. Close your eyes and see if you can determine where the racket is facing after each movement.

You have now taken the first step in learning the forehand drive. This grip may feel strange at first, but with practice, the strangeness will disappear. Avoid the tendency to shift your grip to the right, under the handle. Periodically, go over the description and make any necessary adjustments to return to your original grip.

Backswing

The key to a well-executed stroke is *early preparation,* moving the racket back in anticipation of the forward movement to the ball contact point. This is referred to as the backswing and is similar in preparing for either a forehand or a backhand drive. Several methods may be employed in executing the backswing: a circle or loop, the straight-back pattern, a hairpin, or a semi-loop. The straight-back pattern, lowering the racket head slightly just prior to making the forward swing, is probably the simplest and the one you should master initially.

Regardless of the method you use to take your racket back, it is important to begin the movement as soon as the ball leaves your opponent's racket and you have sensed its direction. The speed with which your racket is drawn back will depend upon the speed of the oncoming ball. Pretend there is a long rod extending from the ball and pushing against the face of your racket. As the ball moves toward you, the rod will force your racket back faster or slower, depending upon the speed of the ball. With practice, you will be able to time the backswing so that the ensuing forward movement occurs without a hitch or pause in the stroke.

The racket is taken back at the predicted height of ball contact. If contact will be at shoulder height, bring the racket back shoulder high; if at waist height,

Ready Position   Backswing: Turn   Backswing: Step

Forward Swing and Point of Impact   Finish

FIGURE 2.3 The forehand drive of the ball with the toe pointing toward the right net post; the head, eyes, left side and shoulder face the net. The knees are flexed for balance.

bring the racket back waist high; if at knee height, *bend your knees* in order to bring the racket back in line with the oncoming ball. Whenever possible, players should attempt to make contact with the ball at hip level since this contact point is most effective anatomically. The following analysis assumes that the approaching ball will be contacted approximately at hip level.

1. From the ready position, begin the backswing by turning your shoulders and hips toward the right sideline. Your hips, shoulders and racket move as one unit. Using the fingers of your left hand to *push* the throat of the racket toward the right sideline may help in initiating the backswing (fig. 2.3).

FIGURE 2.4a Closed, flat or square, and open racket faces

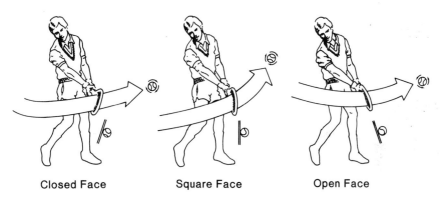

Closed Face   Square Face   Open Face

FIGURE 2.4b Closed, square, and open racket faces

2. As you make the turn, pivot on the ball of your right foot and the ball of your left foot, while transferring your weight to the right foot. Lifting the heel of the left foot allows the left knee to move in toward the right, and the left hip to come around.

3. Continue the backswing of the racket until it is pointing directly at the back fence, slightly lower than hip level. The long strings of the racket remain approximately parallel to the ground. The face of the racket is square or slightly closed (fig. 2.4a, b).

4. As the movement is being completed, your weight is on the back foot (right); move your left foot in the direction of the ball with the toe pointing toward the right net post; the head, eyes, left side and shoulder face the net. The knees are flexed for balance.

5. Extend your left arm away from the body using it as a counterbalance, or point it in the direction of the approaching ball.
6. The upper arm and elbow of the racket hand stay fairly close to your right side, the elbow bent slightly. The wrist is laid back from its ready position to provide opportunity for a slight snap to the stroke during the drive through the ball.

Practice the backswing until the movements become one smooth motion. Begin with the straight backswing and then, if you choose, build in the loop or modified loop by raising the head of the racket at the beginning of the backswing.

Forward Swing to Contact

This is the movement of the racket as it moves forward to intercept the flight of the ball at the point of impact. It will vary with the height of the approaching ball as well as with the position in its trajectory (for example, on the rise, at the top, or as it is coming down—fig. 2.5), at which impact will occur. This description of the forward swing is based on the supposition that the ball has started to drop (after the bounce), and the goal is to make contact at hip level.

1. As the forward swing begins, move the face of the racket so that it is behind and slightly below the expected point of impact. A slight bend of the knees to a modified "sitting positon" may help to keep the racket down.
2. Transfer your weight forward toward the ball by pushing off from your right foot and stepping forward onto your left foot at a forty-five-degree angle to the baseline with the left knee bent. At the same time, begin the forward rotation of the hips and shoulders.
3. As your weight shifts forward and your body pivots, swing your racket forward and upward in a low-to-high path, wrist firm and still laid back, elbow moving away from the body, and arm comfortably extended. Act as though you are attempting to "lift" the ball back over the net.

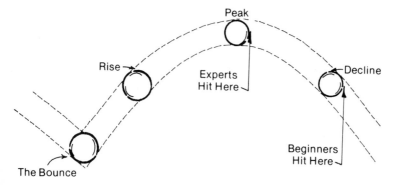

FIGURE 2.5 Ball flight after the bounce: rise, top and descent.

4. The forward swing is fast enough to cause the racket head to "swish" through the air. Continue the stroke through the point of impact toward your intended target. Keep the face of the racket square to the ball as long as possible and keep the racket head vertical, standing on edge.
5. The point of impact is opposite the forward foot. *Watch the ball closely* throughout the stroke and try to see it hit the strings of your racket. Keep your grip and wrist firm on impact by squeezing your fingers just prior to ball contact.
6. The path of the racket begins on an arc and changes to a straight line, thus flattening the arc. This allows you to make slightly early or late contact and still send the ball toward its intended target. Rotating the hips moves them out of the way and helps to straighten the swing (fig. 2.6a, b).

Note: To help visualize the relationship between the ball and the face of the racket on impact, assume that the face of the racket has a pair of eyes (fig. 2.7). Pretend to place your face behind the strings of your racket and look around you, turning your head and your racket simultaneously. Assume that the ball is coming toward you in a fairly level trajectory. When the ball contacts the strings, it will move in the direction toward which the eyes are looking. That is, if the eyes (and racket face) are looking straight ahead, the ball will rebound straight ahead; if the eyes (and the racket face) are looking to the left, the ball will be directed to the left; if facing to the right, the ball will go to the right. This also applies to turning the "eyes" of the racket face down (closed) or up (open) (fig.2.4). Controlling the angle of the racket face at impact is an important factor in directing your shots.

FIGURE 2.6a Flattening the arc

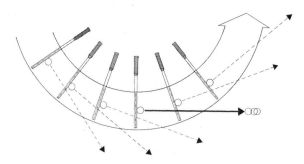

FIGURE 2.6b Swinging along an arc

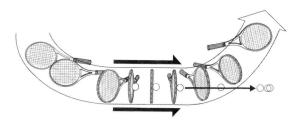

FIGURE 2.6c Swinging along a straight
line

FIGURE 2.7 Eyes on the racket face

Follow-through and Finish

The follow-through is the continuation of the forward swing through the ball in the direction of the intended target. Although research tells us that the ball is on the strings for only four to five milliseconds (.004–.005 ms), the follow-through plays an important part in the full stroke. Attempting to slow the racket down at impact decreases the acceleration of the racket head, a definite factor in the power train. The follow-through lends continuity to the stroke and fluidity to the whole motion, assuring both power and direction. To aid in insuring a good follow-through and in making a good finish:

1. Continue the forward swing of the racket head *through the ball* in the direction of your target.
2. As you make contact, try to keep the racket strings on the ball as long as possible.
3. Let your arm swing across your body, reaching as far as you can toward the target with your racket hand in front of and slightly higher than your left shoulder.
4. Finish the stroke with the racket standing on edge (vertical racket face) pointing up to the top of the opposite fence.
5. Complete your turn so that you are facing the net, hips and shoulders released by lifting the back heel and pivoting on the toe, the toe maintaining contact with the ground. At the completion of the stroke you should be looking over your forearm.
6. Most of your weight is now on the forward foot. Check this by seeing whether you can lift your back foot and still maintain your balance. The forward knee is bent slightly to help maintain that balance and to facilitate a quick return to the ready position.
7. As you complete your turn, resume the hold on the throat of the racket with your left hand and return to the *ready position* for the next shot.

THE BACKHAND DRIVE

The backhand drive is used to contact a ball on the left side of a player's body. It is a necessary, fundamental stroke, just as important as the forehand drive. A correctly executed backhand presents a picture of smoothness and coordination as the racket moves without restriction in the direction of the target. Properly hit, it is just as effective as the forehand. There are only a few basic differences between the forehand and backhand drives. Most of the same principles apply. Both may be practiced and learned simultaneously. Study the directions well, note the comparisons and apply the principles. Like the forehand, the backhand when properly executed is a fluid, continuous motion; for ease and clarity of analysis, it will be presented in its separate parts.

Grip

The following cues will assist you in making the change from the forehand to the backhand grip (Eastern) (fig. 2.8).

1. Support the racket at the throat with the fingers of your left hand, the face of the racket perpendicular to the ground (racket head standing on edge).
2. Start with the forehand grip; then turn your hand and wrist so that the hand moves on top of the grip, the palm facing the top plate. The bottom of the base knuckle of your index finger is squarely on top of the grip.

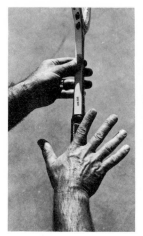

FIGURE 2.8 The backhand grip

3. Close your hand on the grip. The V formed by the thumb and index finger is now on the top left bevel of the grip, and the thumb is diagonally across the back of the grip for added support. Later, you may want to wrap your thumb around the grip. *The fingers are spread slightly.*

The change from the forehand to the backhand grip is made simultaneously with the beginning of the backswing and must be practiced until it becomes automatic. Remember to relax the grip between shots to avoid tiring your hand and arm.

Backswing

As in the forehand, *early preparation* is essential. Turning on the backhand is more pronounced than on the forehand, and the body, at the completion of the backswing, is coiled like a steel spring. With the right hip toward the net, the arm and racket move to a position behind the body. The arm and racket are closer to the body than in the forehand. This analysis assumes that the approaching ball will be contacted at hip height.

1. From the ready position, begin the backswing by turning your shoulders and hips toward the left sideline. Hips, shoulders and racket move as one unit. Use the fingers of your left hand to pull the throat of the racket toward the left sideline; keep the left arm slightly bent (fig. 2.9).
2. As you pull the racket back, make the change from the forehand grip to the backhand grip.
3. As you make the turn, pivot on the ball of the left foot and the ball of the right foot; lifting the heel of the right foot off the ground allows the right knee to move in toward the left.
4. As the backswing continues, the right foot steps across so that the back is half turned toward the net and the toes of the right foot point toward the left net post. The stance is slightly closed, more so than for the forehand.

| Ready Position | Backswing: Turn | Backswing: Step |

Forward Swing and Point of Impact   Finish

FIGURE 2.9 The backhand drive

5. The weight is over the back foot, and the right shoulder is even with or slightly lower than the left. Bend the right knee and relax the shoulders.
6. The right arm hangs down from the shoulder and the elbow is slightly bent. The racket head is pulled back to a position in which the racket hand is a few inches from the left hip. The racket face is square or slightly open.
7. The head and eyes are watching the flight of the ball over the right shoulder while the back of the shoulder faces the net.

Practice the backswing until it becomes a smooth, continuous motion.

Forward Swing to Contact

Following the turn (or preparation), the racket is moved forward, directly into the ball. On balls contacted waist high, the racket face is almost square to the ball. The face is opened slightly for balls lower than the waist in order to lift the ball up and over the net.

1. As the forward swing begins, the head of the racket is raised or lowered to a suitable position for hitting through the ball at its expected height.
2. The weight is shifted forward onto the right foot by pushing from the left foot and bending the right knee.
3. The uncoiling of the hips and shoulders initiates the forward swing of the racket.
4. The hand and racket move away from the hip in the direction of the oncoming ball. The right arm is straightened and brought around the body. The racket head picks up speed (listen for the "swish") as the elbow straightens. The racket head continues its path into and through the ball.
5. Just before impact, the grip tightens on the racket. The ball is contacted six to twelve inches in front of the right foot. Try to watch the ball hit the strings of your racket.
6. As in the forehand, the path of the racket begins on an arc and changes to a straight line (fig. 2.6).

Why should players who are no longer beginners learn to stroke the ball on the rise rather than at its peak?

Follow-through and Finish

As in the forehand, a good follow-through and finish is necessary to give power and direction to the ball. Even though the ball is on the strings for just a fraction of a second, the forward swing, follow-through and finish move the racket face along the line toward the intended target and are important for control. To aid in insuring a good follow-through and in making a good finish:

1. The racket head continues *through the ball* in the direction of the target area.
2. The arm, wrist, hand and racket form a straight line, and the racket head stands on edge.
3. The hips and shoulders remain on line with the intended target.
4. At the finish, the racket hand is at shoulder level or slightly higher. The left arm is extended out away from the body and acts as a counterbalance.
5. The body turn, not as pronounced as in the forehand, is completed. The weight is on the right foot, the right knee slightly bent, with the left toe still in contact with the ground.
6. When the stroke has been completed, return quickly to the ready position, to be prepared for the next shot.

A COMPARATIVE ANALYSIS OF THE FOREHAND AND BACKHAND DRIVES

The following points summarize the similarities and differences in the forehand and backhand drives. Keep these tips in mind during your practice and they will assist you in learning smooth, fluid groundstrokes.

Backhand	Forehand
Ready Position	*Ready Position*
1. Keep your feet comfortably spread, knees bent, back straight, and weight slightly forward.	1. Same as backhand.
2. "Cradle" the racket in your left hand; take a relaxed (not tight) forehand grip on the racket.	2. Same as backhand.
3. Point your racket head in the direction of your opponent.	3. Same as backhand.
4. Relax! But be alert!	4. Same as backhand.
Grip	*Grip*
1. Make certain that you *change* your forehand grip to a backhand grip.	1. Check to be sure that you are holding a forehand grip.
2. Shake hands with your racket so that the *base knuckle* of your index finger is on the top plate.	2. Shake hands with your racket so that the V *between your thumb and index finger* is on the top plate.
3. Keep your fingers spread.	3. Same as backhand.
4. Palm of the hand is on top of the grip (on the *top* plate).	4. Palm of the hand is behind the grip (on the *back* plate).
5. Grip the racket just firmly enough to keep the racket head slightly above the wrist.	5. Same as backhand.
Backswing	*Backswing*
1. Get ready EARLY!	1. Same as backhand.
2. Turn *right* side to the net so *back* of right shoulder points to the net.	2. Turn *left* side to the net so left shoulder points to the net.
3. Use left hand to *pull* the racket to the rear.	3. Use left hand to *push* the racket to the rear.
4. Swing racket head back so it points toward back fence.	4. Swing racket head back so it points *straight back* to the back fence.
5. Shift weight to the rear foot (*left*).	5. Shift weight to the rear foot (*right*).
6. Let arm hang down from shoulder, elbow slightly bent and close to the body.	6. Keep your upper arm fairly close to the body, elbow slightly bent.
7. Keep knees slightly bent.	7. Same as backhand.

Backhand	*Forehand*
Forward Swing	*Forward Swing*
1. Shift weight forward onto the *right* foot while rotating hips and shoulders forward.	1. Shift weight forward onto the *left* foot while rotating hips and shoulders forward.
2. Swing through the ball in a forward, slightly upward motion (from low to high).	2. Same as backhand.
3. With a square racket face contact ball to the side of the body and *in front of* the front foot.	3. With a square racket face contact ball to the side of the body and *opposite* the front foot.
4. Flatten the arc of your swing.	4. Same as backhand.
5. Keep the strings on the ball as long as possible.	5. Same as backhand.
Follow-through and Finish	*Follow-through and Finish*
1. Swing your racket through the ball in the direction of your intended target.	1. Same as backhand.
2. Finish stroke with racket high, "standing on edge," pointing at the opposite fence.	2. Same as backhand.
3. Recover quickly to your ready position.	3. Same as backhand.

Standing in the ready position, shift your grip back and forth between the backhand and forehand positions without looking at the racket. After every third shift, check to see whether your racket hand is accurately placed.

When you have practiced and learned both the forehand and backhand stroke patterns independently, continue your practice by alternating strokes; i.e., start in an active ready position, stroke through the forehand pattern, return to the ready position, stroke through the backhand pattern, return to the ready position and so on. Use this is a warm-up exercise prior to play.

THE TWO-HANDED BACKHAND

In recent years, increasing television exposure to Tracy Austin, Bjorn Borg, Jimmy Connors and Chris Evert Lloyd has created an interest in the two-handed backhand. Regardless of age or skill level, many players and spectators want to know more about how the experts hit their two-handed shots, as well as the pros and cons of various techniques.

In hitting a backhand drive, do you:
1. Change your grip? Place base knuckle of the index finger on the top plate?
*2. Watch the ball until **after** contact?*
*3. Turn so the **back** of your right shoulder is toward the net?*
4. Swing level, or just slightly from low to high?
*5. Contact the ball **ahead** of your front foot? Have a slightly open racket face?*
6. Follow through out in the direction of the target?

A two-handed backhand has both advantages and disadvantages. Among the advantages of the two-handed shot are the ability to disguise the shot, along with increased ability to hit sharp and zipping crosscourt passing shots. Having two hands on the racket produces a more compact and stronger swing, allowing players with weak arms and wrists to overcome that handicap by using both arms together. The two-handed stroke usually follows a low-to-high movement path, thus enhancing the application of topspin and the ability to play balls approaching at a low level; conversely, the application of slice and backspin is more difficult, and high bouncing balls can be the two-hander's nemesis. A player cannot reach as far with two hands as with one, and this reduced reach requires the player to have quicker reactions and/or more speed in order to take the necessary additional step. Many people are finding increased success utilizing a two-handed backhand and you may be one of them. Those interested in this possibility should read on!

Grip(s)

Note the *s* within the parentheses of the heading! There are probably as many variations of two-handed grips as there are people using the two-handed stroke. Some players use an interlocking grip, similar to the type used in golf; others use a double forehand grip. Probably the best combination is the one used by both Austin and Borg—certainly they are excellent role models and their approach seems to be the most sound mechanically. This grip utilizes a backhand (Eastern or Continental) grip with the right hand and forehand (Eastern) grip with the left hand, thus providing an important safety device for those occasions when you cannot get close enough to the ball to hit your two-handed shot; since you will have a backhand grip with your right hand, you will be able to hit some kind of a one-hand backhand return.

Assuming that you hold a forehand grip in the ready position, switch to the backhand as you start your backswing. Slide the left hand down the handle to the forehand grip as shown in the photograph (fig. 2.10). Keep your hands close together and grip the racket firmly.

FIGURE 2.10 The two-handed backhand grip

Backswing

The backswing in the two-handed backhand is very similar to that used in the conventional backhand drive (see preceding section). Preparation for the two-handed shot will require the player to move a little closer to the line of flight of the approaching ball. In addition, the body turn may be accentuated and the racket head points slightly downward behind the left hip (fig. 2.11). Practice moving from the ready position to the end of the backswing until the sequence becomes smooth and continuous.

Ready Position   Backswing: Turn   Backswing: Step

Forward Swing and Point of Impact   Finish

FIGURE 2.11 The two-handed backhand

Forward Swing to Contact

The forward swing and contact are accomplished by a step to the ball and an uncoiling of the hips and shoulders. The weight is shifted forward and both arms swing around and through the ball. Ball contact is closer to, but still out in front of, the body. The path of the swing goes from low to high, and the face of the racket controls the direction and trajectory of the ball.

Follow-through and Finish

Again these actions are very similar to those utilized in the conventional backhand, except that both hands move the racket through the ball and finish at shoulder level, arms fully extended. A more flamboyant type may wind up the shot by bending both elbows, thus allowing the racket head to be wrapped spectacularly around the neck! Leave that stuff to the pros, concentrate on a solid contact and normal follow-through. Your return to the ready position will be considerably quicker and you will not be caught gawking at a quick return from your opponent.

Two-handed Backhand Reminders

The following suggestions will help you learn the two-handed backhand:

1. Move into position quickly and take your racket well back in preparation.
2. Get your side to the net and get close enough to the ball so your forward swing can make solid contact.
3. Make contact well in front of your body.
4. Hit firmly through the ball.
5. Swing from low to high as you hit the ball to provide a little topspin.

In deciding whether to use the two-handed backhand, what advantages and disadvantages should be considered?

FOOTWORK

Since the ball will rarely come to you in perfect position to be hit, you must move into position to hit the ball. Footwork is one of the most important fundamentals of tennis, as well as for any sport that involves movement, such as basketball, soccer, or handball. Good footwork gets you into the best possible position from which to execute your shots and greatly facilitates that execution. Poor footwork causes you to hit late, from awkward, off-balance positions, making easy shots more difficult and hard shots almost impossible. Watch a good player. Much of the grace and ease of execution may be attributed to proper movement on the court. An old saying that "the average player waits for the ball while the expert *moves to the ball*" is certainly evident in championship tennis.

Now that you have learned how to execute the strokes correctly, you are ready to combine execution with movement. The following suggestions will be helpful in improving your footwork:

1. When waiting for the return, assume an active, balanced ready position, prepared to move quickly in any direction (fig. 2.1).
2. *As soon as* the ball leaves your opponent's racket and you determine the direction of the approaching ball, *you must begin to move.*
3. When moving only a short distance to your right, left, or diagonally forward, move the foot nearest the ball first to slide, turn, and step forward to the ball. Follow the pattern in figure 2.12 for the forehand: (1) STEP to the side with your right foot; (2) SLIDE your left foot beside your right; (3) TURN and STEP again on your right foot; and (4) STEP FORWARD on your left foot to contact the ball. Your first step is accompanied by a turn of the hips and shoulders, thus initiating the backswing. At the completion of the TURN-STEP (3), your weight should be on your back foot and your racket should point to the back fence, ready to stroke the ball. When stepping forward (4) to the ball, you may use a large or small step, wide, straight ahead, or diagonally forward, to place yourself in perfect position to stroke the oncoming ball. Pushing off on the balls of the feet contributes to a quicker start. For the backhand, the pattern is reversed. Practice walking through both patterns.
4. For a ball landing deep in the court (fig. 2.13): (1) TURN and step back with your right foot (forehand) or left foot (backhand); (2) SLIDE your other foot back; and (3) STEP BACK again. At the completion of the turn, your racket should be back ready to stroke the ball. After completing (3), your weight will be on your rear foot; remember to change direction and shift your weight forward as you make the forward swing.

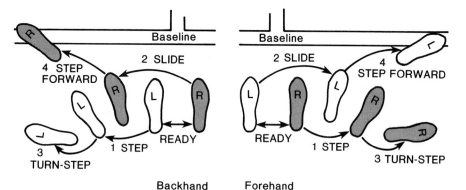

Backhand   Forehand

FIGURE 2.12 Footwork for short moves to the side: remember to change direction and shift your weight forward as you make the forward swing.

5. For a ball that will land short (fig. 2.14): (1) TURN and step forward with your left foot (forehand) or your right foot (backhand); (2) SLIDE your other foot forward; and (3) STEP FORWARD again. This is the two-step or step-together-step pattern that is also useful in making final adjustments for any stroke.

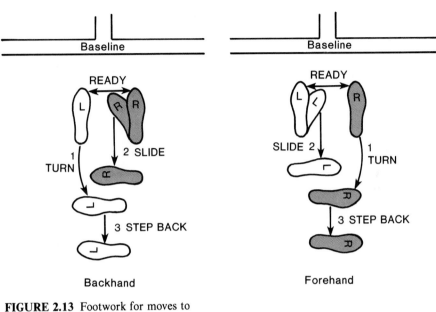

FIGURE 2.13 Footwork for moves to the rear

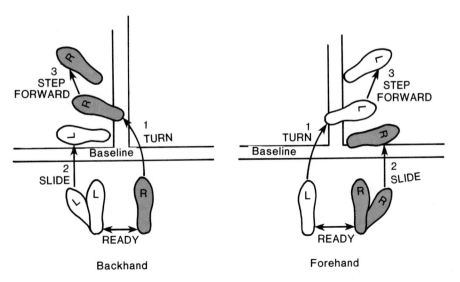

FIGURE 2.14 Footwork for moving forward

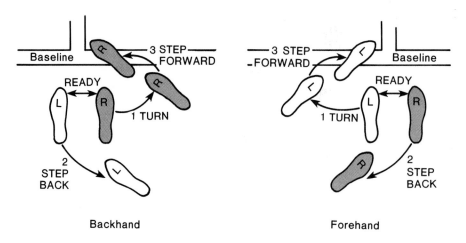

Backhand   Forehand

FIGURE 2.15 Footwork for shots
coming directly at you

6. If a ball is hit directly at you, and you wish to hit a forehand drive (fig. 2.15):
   (1) TURN and move your left foot to the left; (2) STEP BACK, swinging
   your right foot around to the rear; and (3) STEP FORWARD with your left
   foot to stroke the ball. If you feel more confident using a backhand (fig.
   2.15): (1) TURN and move your right foot to the right; (2) STEP BACK,
   swinging your left foot around to the rear; and (3) STEP FORWARD with
   your right foot to stroke the ball.
7. When running greater distances (fig. 2.16a, b) it is more efficient and faster
   to (1) CROSS OVER with the foot farthest from the ball. Move quickly,
   taking longer steps at first, then smaller steps and finally (5) STEP FOR-
   WARD to stroke the ball. If necessary, make slight adjustments by using a
   little skip or two-step (step-together-step, fig. 2.14). Prepare for the stroke
   as you run, moving the racket part of the way around and completing the
   backswing with the planting of the forward foot.
8. When running for a ball, avoid charging directly into it. Move to a position
   15 to 20 feet behind and alongside the spot where the ball will hit the ground,
   and stop! In catching a ball a player would get into position directly behind
   the line-of-flight of the ball. In stroking a tennis ball, the length of the arm
   and racket allows you to be to one side of the line-of-flight, much like a
   baseball batter who stands beside home plate instead of behind it.
9. Immediately after making your shot, slide or run quickly back to your basic
   position behind the center mark to assume an active ready position awaiting
   your opponent's return.

Practice each of the described movements separately and then put them together
into a series. Use music to help develop an easy, rhythmical motion and you will
soon find yourself moving quickly, easily, and more efficiently on the court.

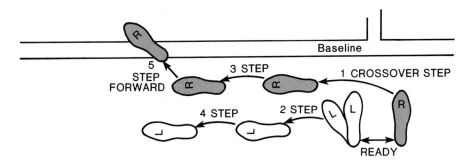

Backhand

FIGURE 2.16a Footwork for covering
greater distances

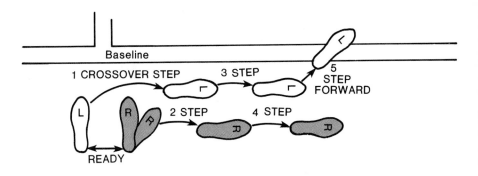

Forehand

FIGURE 2.16b Footwork for covering
greater distances

THE SERVE

The serve is the stroke that puts the ball in play and is often referred to as the
most important stroke in the game of tennis. It has become a principle weapon
of attack and is used to place the opponent on the defensive by forcing a return
from the weak side or by moving the receiver out of position. A strong serve may
bolster an otherwise weak game and tends to build the server's confidence.

Because both hands are in motion at the same time (ball toss and racket
arm), coordination may be difficult for the beginner. To a point, serving is like
throwing a baseball overhand; however, in addition to the throwing motion, the
placement of the ball in the hitting position (ball toss) introduces another element. The serve requires the coordination of those two movements to bring the
ball and racket into position for the most effective contact.

Grip

The grip taught to most beginners is the forehand grip since it has already been learned. However, it is advisable to move to the conventional service grip, halfway between the forehand and backhand, as soon as possible. Some beginners are able to start with this service grip, called the Continental grip. More advanced players will find it gives them greater flexibility in hitting the various serves, i.e., flat, slice, topspin or American twist. In the service grip, the bottom of the base knuckle of the index finger lies on the top back bevel. The fingers are spread and the thumb is wrapped around the handle. The grip is relaxed, not tight. As a beginner, you may wish to hold the grip more with the palm of the hand, much like the forehand; this will give you more control. As an advanced player, the racket is held primarily with the fingers to allow the wrist the flexibility that is necessary to produce increased speed.

Stance

When serving to the right service court, take a position sideways to the net three or four feet to the right of the center mark behind the baseline. The left foot is two to three inches behind the line, the toes pointing toward the right net post. The back foot is parallel to the baseline and spread comfortably (about 18″) from the front foot. For the time being, the weight is primarily on the back foot. An extension of a line drawn through the toes of both feet should point to the target (fig. 2.17).

Take the Continental grip on the racket and cradle the racket at its throat with the fingers of the left hand; the elbows are fairly close to the body. The racket head is tilted up and points in the intended direction of the serve. The

FIGURE 2.17 Stance for the serve

fingers cradling the racket are also holding one or two balls (fig. 2.18). The entire body is poised but not tense. *Relaxation* and *balance* are extremely important. The hand and arm holding the racket are especially loose.

Keep the toes of the left foot in contact with the ground throughout the serve, moving the foot only after contact has been made and the momentum of the racket pulls you into the court. Keeping the foot on the ground will give you a firm base from which to hit and at the same time will eliminate possible foot faults.

Ball Toss

The ball toss is the key to a well-executed serve; a good release consistently places the ball in the proper hitting position. A poor release spells trouble and is often the cause of a poor serve.

The balls are held in the fingers of the left hand, palm up. The ball to be tossed is held by the thumb, index and middle fingers. If a second ball is held, it is pressed against the heel of the hand by the third and fourth fingers. The ball is "placed" in the air (not thrown) by an extension of the arm and hand, ending in full extension forward of the right shoulder. The ball should be tossed with little or no spin. Keeping the fingers extended will prevent "hooking" the toss which leads to loss of control. The ball is tossed in the direction of the right net post (in the direction the forward foot is pointed) to a height slightly higher than the combined reach of the arm and racket. If the toss were allowed to drop, it would land in the court, approximately 18 inches in front of the right shoulder.

Imagine that the ball has a face on it, looking directly at you. For the flat serve, the ball is tossed in front of the right shoulder and hit on the "nose"; for a slice serve, the ball is tossed to the right and the racket hits the "left eye" of the ball; and for a topspin serve, the ball is tossed over the player's head and the

FIGURE 2.18 Serve grip and ball hold

FIGURE 2.19 Ball toss and racket face
angle for three types of serves:
American twist (topspin), slice, flat

racket face moves from the "nose" up and over the "left eye" (fig. 2.19). Whatever the type of serve, the toss must be appropriate and consistent. Control of
the ball toss cannot be overemphasized. Trouble comes from tosses that are too
high, too low, too quick, or too inconsistent. Inconsistency in the toss is almost
always accompanied by an inconsistent serve. Practice the ball toss correctly and
often, and you will find your serve improving. According to the rules, you don't
have to swing at a bad toss—so don't!

The serve, like the groundstrokes, is presented one step at a time. The grip,
stance, and ball toss have been described. Of equal and perhaps more importance
is the simultaneous action of the serving arm—the actual "weapon." The first
movement, coordinated with the ball toss, is the *backswing,* the downward-upward
or drawing action of the arm and racket; second, the *upward-forward swing* into
the point of contact; and finally, the *follow-through and finish* (fig. 2.20).

Backswing

As the ball toss begins, the right arm and racket begin the downward swing with
the edge of the racket head leading. The left and right arms move downward and
upward in unison (down together-up together). The ball is released just before
the left arm reaches full extension. The racket head begins an arc that starts in
front and slightly to the right of the body, continues downward, back, and upward
behind the back to a position over the head. When the elbow reaches a position
slightly higher than the shoulder, the elbow bends and the racket head drops
down behind the back into what is commonly called the "back-scratching position," the racket head pointing straight down to the ground. The trunk and shoulders have rotated away from the net. At this time, the ball should be at the top

FIGURE 2.20 The serve

of the toss. This part of the motion is slow and deliberate, like an archer drawing a bow or the coiling of a steel spring. What follows is the explosive upward-forward motion of the racket into ball contact.

Practice the down together-up together coordination of the ball toss and racket arms (keeping the palm of the tossing hand up) until it is smooth and consistent.

Forward Swing to Contact

As the ball starts down, the weight shifts forward, the shoulders and trunk rotate forward, the wrist and elbow "snap" the racket head upward and forward, contacting the ball with the body, arm, and racket at full extension. The edge of the racket, rather than the face, moves to the ball, opening slightly as it approaches the contact point. This results in an outward pronation of the hand and wrist, a natural motion (fig. 2.21).

Contrary to what you may believe, the racket should not hit down on the ball—even if you are extremely tall. The racket moves upward and outward, a motion that will bring the ball down into the court and still impart a forward penetrating bounce after landing. The movement described here is similar to that of throwing a ball across the net with an overhand motion. The ball is struck just as it starts to drop, and the racket head should be moving so rapidly that you can hear it "swish" through the air. Making contact with the racket face square to the ball (on the "nose") will result in a flat serve (fig. 2.19). Brushing outward and contacting the side of the ball causes it to spin on its vertical axis from right to left, or *slice* (see chapter 3).

Make sure you keep your chin up and *watch the ball closely* until the follow-through has begun. The body should not "jackknife" or bend sharply at the waist before or during the serve.

If allowed to drop, a good ball toss for the flat serve would land in the court about 18 inches in front of the right shoulder. Out of 10 tries of tossing the ball as the racket arm swings back, are your direction and distance good 6 times, 8 times, 9 times, 10 times?

FIGURE 2.21 Outward pronation of the wrist

Follow-through and Finish

Again, the follow-through is up and out (not down) in the direction of the intended target area and is a natural continuation of the stroke. It continues with the head of the racket swinging freely past the left side of the body. The right foot swings across the baseline and continues forward, taking a step in the direction of the serve to help maintain balance and continue your momentum. Later it will become the first step in your approach to the net (fig. 2.20). The left arm moves backward, aiding in body rotation and maintaining balance.

The serve is important; therefore, spend as much time as you can to perfect it. Learn to serve from both sides of the court and get into the habit of deciding where and how you want the ball to go every time you serve. Make certain you have loosened your shoulder joint and muscles with good stretches and by hitting easy preliminary serves, prior to your service practice. Avoid shoulder injury by practicing good serving habits.

Serve Reminders

Use the following suggestions to assist you in learning the serve:

1. Take your stance at the baseline and check to make certain that a line through your toes points in the direction of your serve.
2. Point your left foot toward the right net post.
3. Start with your weight on your back foot.
4. Grip the racket primarily with your fingers.
5. Hold your racket in front of your body and point it toward your target area.
6. Look to be sure the receiver is ready; take a deep breath.
7. Use a smooth tossing motion to place the ball in the hitting zone. Palm up!
8. Toss the ball toward the right net post.
9. Think—"down together-up together."
10. Drop the racket head down behind your back, then . . .
11. Hit up and out—over the ball.
12. Keep your chin up—watch the ball closely!
13. Relax: try not to overpower the ball; let the speed of the racket head do the work.
14. Swing slow on the bottom—fast on top.
15. Transfer your weight from your back to your front foot; rotate the trunk and shoulders forward.
16. Follow through!

RETURN OF SERVE

The return of serve is probably the least practiced stroke yet one of the most important to the game. Unless your opponent's serve can be returned, the point is lost—you have no chance of winning it. Consequently, even in the early stages of learning to play tennis, the beginning and intermediate player needs to understand how to apply basic principles (many of which you already know!) to this situation.

First of all, the return of serve is a groundstroke, since the serve must bounce in the proper service court. Review the mechanics of the ready position, as well as the forehand and backhand drives. Generally, the best position for returning serve is behind the baseline, near the singles sideline. Assume an active ready position—be alert. Adjust the speed of your backswing to the speed of the on-coming serve. To return harder, faster serves, move your ready position back a step or two and use a short, straight backswing; there will not be time for one of your long, flowing, beautiful groundstrokes! In order to return softer, slower serves move in a step or two, and you should have time for your normal backswing. More advanced analysis is presented in Chapter 3 and strategy considerations are discussed in Chapter 5; but at any skill level and above all else, *be alert and concentrate on getting the ball back and in play!*

THE VOLLEY

The volley is the stroke used to hit the ball after it clears the net and before it contacts the ground. It is usually hit from a position near the net; however, it can be made from almost anywhere on the court. Although it is not necessary to be able to volley to play tennis, lack of volleying skill will limit the offensive potential of a player. At some time or another, you will find yourself near the net with the opportunity to volley the return for a winner. Players who purposely stay at the baseline give their opponents an edge, even though they may be excellent baseline players. Unless they are exceptional, they put little or no pressure on their opponents and willingly give up the strong net position to the other side. Doubles play is built around the serve and volley and volleying is definitely a part of the "big game" that is the trademark of many of today's champions. Besides all these important tactical considerations, volleying is fun! It is easy to learn, especially after a reasonable amount of practice. So, read on, and practice!

To be effective, the shot is made from above net height where it can be hit downward for a winner. If the ball is contacted below the level of the net, the volley becomes a defensive shot and must be hit up to clear the net. This may set it up for your opponent who is waiting for a high ball that can be put away for a winner. The volley movement is similar to a punch or block, and it does not have the long sweep of the groundstrokes. Since both forehand and backhand volleys are very similar, they are discussed together.

Grip

The grips are the same as those used for the groundstrokes, the Eastern forehand (fig. 2.2) and Eastern backhand (fig. 2.8). As your tennis experience increases, you may prefer to use the Continental grip described in the section on the serve. The Eastern grips are preferable for most beginners while the Continental grip is used by many advanced players. The following descriptions are based on the Eastern grips.

Stance

The basic volleying position is about six to eight feet away from the net. The ready position is the same as for the groundstrokes, except that the head of the racket is raised slightly, to approximately eye level. Look past the head of your racket to see the oncoming ball. This keeps the volleyer's racket in position to make a quick backswing in preparation for either a forehand or a backhand volley.

Backswing

There is little or no backswing in most volleys; in general, the shorter the better, especially for punch volleys directed at hard-hit balls. At the end of the backswing, the head of the racket should be visible out of the corner of your eye, within your peripheral vision. For a ball approaching slowly (a soft or weak return), it may be necessary to increase the length of the backswing and to turn the shoulders more so as to gain added power—a volley made with a long backswing is referred to as a drive volley. For a ball approaching rapidly, the backswing may be no more than a slight turn of the shoulders. Usually, the shoulder turn is combined with a step *toward the ball* with the lead foot (left foot for forehand volleys, right foot for backhand volleys) (fig. 2.22).

For a ball approaching at shoulder height, the head of the racket is halfway between the horizontal and vertical positions. The racket head is on a diagonal, the elbow bent. As the body turn is made, the racket is pulled back to a position behind the spot where you intend to meet the ball. Bend the wrist back slightly and lock it to eliminate wrist movement on the forward swing.

For the backhand volley, the grip (Eastern) is changed at the beginning of the shoulder turn and the racket is guided back with both hands (fig. 2.23). The left hand releases the racket at the beginning of the forward swing. Take the racket back by bending the left elbow, thus lifting the racket head above the wrist, and bringing the racket head back even with the front shoulder. As in the forehand, the wrist is locked and the racket head is in position directly behind the intended contact point.

For a ball coming directly at you to the middle of your body, the backhand volley is used as an effective and protective shot. The right elbow lifts and the racket head drops into a horizontal position in front of the body. For balls approaching slightly to the right of center, the volleyer steps or leans to the left and makes a forehand volley. The reverse holds true for balls hit slightly to the left of center.

How does the ready position for volleying differ from the position for receiving groundstrokes? When and why may it be necessary to lengthen the backswing for a volley contacted above net level?

Practice the preparation for a volley until your backswing becomes automatic. The shoulder turn, the footwork, the grip change, the racket movement for balls approaching at various heights, on both sides and right at you should become automatic.

Ready Position	Turn	Step
Hit	Contact Well in Front	Finish

FIGURE 2.22 The forehand volley

Forward Swing to Contact

The forward swing to the point of contact is very brief and compact, sometimes only a matter of inches. Use an arm and shoulder motion to move the racket head forward in a slightly descending path to meet the ball with a punching or blocking type of movement. Whenever possible (if you have time), *step forward* to provide for the transfer of weight, which is especially important in the volley since the backswing is limited. Keep your knees bent.

The ball is contacted *well out in front,* and whenever possible, to the side of the body. Squeeze your fingers around the grip just before impact to help keep the wrist firm at contact. The forward movement of the racket is accompanied by the positioning of the racket face. Keep in mind the "eyes" on the racket

Ready Position	Turn	Step

Hit	Contact Well in Front	Finish

FIGURE 2.23 The backhand volley

described earlier (fig. 2.7). The ball goes where the "eyes" are looking. Contacting the ball earlier or later also contributes to the direction of the volley. In general, a laid-back wrist will result in a down-the-line volley, while straightening the wrist and the racket will result in a crosscourt return.

On the backhand side, the lowering and raising of the elbow away from the body will alter the face of the racket and influence the direction of the volley. Although the elbow remains bent in the forehand volley, the elbow, on the backhand volley, *straightens* as the racket moves to the contact point.

There are occasions when it is necessary to volley from below the level of the net. To accomplish this effectively, bend your knees (not your waist), open the racket face (make the "eyes" look up), and direct the ball over the net with a slight lifting motion; contact the bottom half of the ball well out in front. The amount of racket slant will depend on your distance from the net; the closer, the more the face must open. Step forward to give impetus to the ball.

Follow-through and Finish

There is a slight follow-through in the direction of the placement with the racket face remaining square to the ball. Limit the extent of the volley so that a blocking or punching motion is used and a short follow-through will result. Return to the ready position immediately.

In hitting a volley, do you:

1. *Keep sight of your racket during the backswing?*
2. *Punch the ball, using a minimum stroke?*
3. *Keep your wrist firm on impact?*
4. *Meet the ball **well out in front** of you?*
5. *Keep your racket head above your wrist?*
6. *Bend your knees for low balls?*

Volley Reminders

Use the following checkpoints while practicing and learning the volley:

1. Prepare early by being on your toes, racket head up, ready to meet the ball.
2. Look past your racket head in the direction of the oncoming ball.
3. Start the backswing with your shoulder turn—keep it short and simple!
4. Place your racket head behind the intended point of contact to intercept the ball.
5. Step *forward* to meet the ball *well out in front of* and to the side of your body.
6. Cross your feet—left foot forward for a forehand; right foot forward for a backhand.
7. Block or punch the ball, keeping your follow-through short.
8. Squeeze your fingers around the grip to make your wrist firm.
9. For low balls, drop your knees not your racket head!
10. Return to the ready position quickly!

Now that you know how to SERVE the ball to start the point, RETURN SERVE to get the ball back in play, continue the point with proper GROUND-STROKES, and advance to the net to VOLLEY the ball for a winner, it is important that you solidify these newly-acquired strokes through PURPOSEFUL PRACTICE. Consult Chapter 4 for practice suggestions to help speed your progress.

3 Better Players Master These Strokes

Now that you have mastered the essential tennis strokes, you will want to focus your practice on what are often referred to as auxiliary strokes. These are variations of the basic strokes that are used by more advanced players either to win a point outright or to maneuver an opponent out of position, thereby setting up a winning shot. By this time you will have become aware of the differences in playing styles, the fact that individual players play the game differently. They hold the racket differently, their preparations vary, their swings vary and their personalities vary. In other words, even though you do not develop the classic strokes described in Chapter 2, you may still develop a strong and perhaps even a championship style of your own.

The following paragraphs describe some of the advanced techniques necessary to move you through the intermediate and advanced stages of your game. Look for them when you are watching championship play—work on them in practice!

BALL SPIN

There is probably no such thing as a perfectly "flat" drive or serve in tennis. Some degree of spin occurs each time the ball is hit. The flat stroke refers to a ball hit squarely with a relatively level swing, as contrasted with the overspin and underspin drives described in the following paragraphs.

An understanding of ball spin is necessary before you can begin mastering the auxiliary strokes. Understanding spin and the effect it has on the flight and bounce of the ball will assist you in varying your stroke production and in preparing for groundstroke and service returns. When you are able to *control* ball spin and can also play the spinning ball after it bounces, you will be well on your way toward achieving a well-rounded game.

A simple approach to understanding the effects of spin on the ball is to remember that a spinning ball moves in the direction of its rotation. Therefore, a ball that is spinning forward tends to drop; a ball spinning backward tends to rise; and a ball spinning sideways tends to curve left or right. Each of these spins is presented separately.

Topspin (Forward Spin, Overspin, or Loop)

Several methods are used to impart topspin to the ball. Some, like the wrist roll, require a strong wrist and should be left to players like Rod Laver or Bjorn Borg. To develop good topspin, the basic approach is to start the racket head from a position behind and below the ball with either a slightly closed or square racket face. Move the racket head forward and upward through the ball, keeping the face perpendicular to the intended line of flight. Continue upward after contact, finishing high and in front of your body. The same principle applies to both the forehand and the backhand; that is, start your racket head lower than your intended point of contact and complete the follow-through with a high finish. The amount of topspin may be controlled by varying the angle of your low-to-high swing; that is, the greater the angle, the greater the spin.

The ball spins in the direction of the stroke and, when coupled with the forces of gravity and air resistance, drops swiftly to the ground. As a result of the overspin, the ball travels faster after the bounce than before—it shoots forward and upward. Because of the sharp drop of the ball during its flight (it seems to dip downward), this shot is used against a net rusher, thus forcing a volley or half volley played defensively from below the top of the net.

The application of topspin to groundstrokes provides a greater margin of error since the shot crosses the net higher than the typical flat shot and drops sharply within the baseline. This permits the player to hit the ball harder while still retaining control. Figure 3.1 assumes that the topspin shot (C) is hit harder than the backspin shot (A) or the flat shot (B). Various topspins are also used when serving and will be discussed in a later section.

Backspin

Backspin is the reverse of topspin. The ball, after being hit, turns away from the direction in which it is moving. To achieve backspin, the racket head starts from

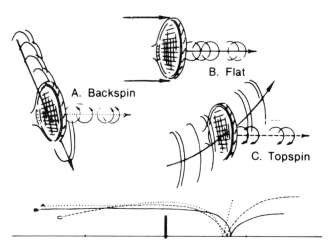

FIGURE 3.1 Ball spin

a position behind and *above* the ball, strikes the backside and continues down and through the ball (high to low); adjust the face of the racket to control the amount of spin. The greater the high-to-low angle and the slant of the racket face, the greater the backspin.

Backspin causes the ball to rise slightly after contact, thus producing a floating type of flight. When the ball hits the ground, it loses much of its forward momentum. It may either "hug" the ground or bounce sharply upward, depending on the amount of spin (chop, chip, slice) and the angle at which it approaches the ground. The backspin return is used both offensively and defensively; it is especially useful for high backhand returns, low volleys, and approach shots. In general, the slice is used primarily to maintain control of the ball and to keep it in play.

Sidespin

Although not as popular, sidespin is used by some players when hitting down-the-line shots or when using an extreme slice on the serve. When hitting a slice, the ball is made to turn on its vertical axis by stroking across the ball, either left-to-right or right-to-left, making it spin like a top. The ball will move in the direction of its rotation, and for this reason is used frequently on approach shots and serves to force an opponent wide, thereby opening up the court for a winning placement.

THE ADVANCED SERVES

The serve must be varied to keep your opponent from getting set and grooving the return. Variation may occur by changing speed, spin, or direction. Once you have mastered the beginner's flat serve, you must move ahead and learn the *slice* and *topspin* serves. With them you will be ready to go on the offensive and at the same time make your delivery more consistent. Like the baseball pitcher who throws curves as well as fastballs, you will keep the receiver (batter) off balance.

The Slice Serve

The slice is similar to the flat serve. Just a few slight differences in technique produce the slice or sliding effect. The service grip (Continental) described earlier, halfway between the forehand (fig. 2.2) and backhand grips (fig. 2.8), is more flexible and is designed for advanced serves. Keep the same ball toss you learned earlier, i.e., toss it in the direction of the right net post, a little higher than you can reach with your arm and racket extended, so that if the ball were permitted to drop to the ground, it would bounce about a foot inside the baseline, in front of the right shoulder. The knees bend and the back arches in preparation for the upward-forward swing into the ball. The racket face strikes the ball on the upper right section and around the outside of the ball; this causes the ball to rotate sideways or slice in the direction of the left sideline. The follow-through is out, a little to the right of the intended direction of the serve, and the finish is the same. Once more, it's important that you "keep your chin up" and watch the ball throughout.

The slice serve is used primarily to draw the receiver wide and off the court, keeping the ball down. It is also used to spin the ball into the receiver's body, thereby forcing a more difficult return. It may be used in singles and doubles for the first and/or the second serve. Once mastered, you can rely on it to make your serve more consistent for you and more unpredictable for your opponent.

The Topspin Serve

The topspin serve, sometimes called the twist or American twist, is difficult to learn and should not be seriously attempted until both the flat and slice services have been mastered. Nevertheless, it must be learned if you are to complete your "service arsenal." Use the Continental grip, or you may wish to try the Eastern backhand grip. The ball is tossed (*placed*) above your left shoulder, or a few inches in front of your head (see fig. 2.19). The body is arched and the knees bent, the racket head drops behind the back and the wrist is cocked. With your body coiled, initiate the upward-forward swing by straightening your body and leaning forward into the shot. Just before impact, straighten your wrist sharply so that the face of the racket hits the ball in an upward brushing motion, similar to that used in hitting the topspin groundstroke. Your elbow is still bent on contact, but straightens as you bring the racket head up and over the ball. The direction of the racket, basically from left to right, may be changed to produce a variety of spins on the ball. Swing out and away from your body and continue with your normal follow-through and finish. You will find that your racket follows a more outward path on the topspin serve than the more forward path of both the slice and flat serves. The topspin serve will break down and out to make the ball bounce high and break away from the receiver's backhand. It allows a greater margin for error and is used primarily as a second serve in singles. Like the slice, it can keep the receiver off balance and at the same time give the server more time to move in to the net. It is especially useful against players who have weak backhand returns or who cannot handle high balls well.

It is important for you to work equally hard on both first and second serves. Learn to hit both serves with equal force and similar motions. Remember, you can use more force when hitting with topspin and still keep the ball in the court. A poorly hit topspin serve may tend to sit up and give the receiver an opportunity to move in and hit a forcing return. However, one of the advantages of a well-hit topspin serve is that you don't have to "ease up" on your second serve; thus you can keep your opponent on the defense.

With which type of spin should you stroke the ball if you wish to draw your opponent toward the net (drop shot)? Toward the baseline? Toward the left sideline?

RETURN OF SERVE

As you gain skill and experience, you will come to realize how very important the return of serve is. A good return of serve will take the offensive edge away from the server and swing it in your favor. You must be able to break serve in order to win the match; and returning the serve—just getting the ball back and in play—gives you a fifty-fifty chance of winning the point.

Review again the basics presented in Chapter 2; then study and practice the suggestion presented here. The server determines when and how the ball will be served; as the receiver, you must be prepared for anything that comes. The rules (see chapter 6) permit the receiver to take any position desired, so strategy and skill should dictate your position. Strategy is discussed in Chapter 5, and skill is considered here. In determining your best receiving position, you must analyze the serve of your opponent: What kind of serve is it—flat? slice? topspin? How consistent is it? What difference is there between the first and second serves? What targets can the server hit—near the center line? wide? right at you? In addition to these questions, you must ask yourself: How good is my return? Can I play the high bouncing serve on the rise? Can I block a fast serve back from inside the baseline? How well do I handle the wide serve? The answers to both sets of questions will help you to determine your receiving position and your shot selection. The return of serve is not just one stroke; any number of strokes (i.e., forehand, backhand, lob, drop shot), hit with a variety of spins and/or speeds, to a variety of targets (deep corners, short corners, crosscourt, down-the-line) can be utilized. The smart receiver selects shots well within his or her capabilities, which will attack the server's weaknesses.

Return of Serve Reminders

1. Assume a *dynamic* ready position—relax while waiting, but be alert.
2. *Adjust your position* up, back, and sideways, depending on the type of serve anticipated and whether it is a first or second serve. Your stance should bisect the angle of your opponent's serving range. Move inside the baseline to play high-bouncing topspin serves on the rise, before the spin moves you off the court.
3. Turn your shoulders as soon as you know the direction of the serve, get ready early, shift your weight forward, keep a firm grip, contact the ball out in front of your body, follow through the shot. Use a slice to return high-bouncing topspin serves; use a short backswing to block back high-speed serves.
4. If the ball is served wide, move *diagonally forward* to intercept ball flight as soon as possible; if you stay behind the baseline and move laterally only, the serve will draw you well off the court.
5. Before the serve is delivered, *have a plan;* know what type of return you will attempt to make. If the server surprises you with an unanticipated serve, you'll have to scramble, but as you gain skill in analyzing the server's patterns, you will be surprised less often.
6. Decide on the target for your return, based on what the server does after the serve. If the server stays back, make your returns high and deep to keep your opponent back behind the baseline; if the server follows the serve to the net, chip short and wide returns aimed crosscourt at the short corner, or hit a topspin return to the same target to force the server to hit difficult volleys or half volleys.

7. Immediately after your return, be on your way to a strategic ready position in anticipation of the next shot. Do not stand there admiring the marvelous artistic return you have just made. Get going!

Where should you stand to receive high-bouncing topspin serves and what kind of stroke makes an effective return against such serves?

Keep the pressure on the server by making a high percentage of your returns. Do not give away "free points" through loose or careless play when a return could result in a winner for you. Get the ball back and give your opponent the chance to make an error. Set up situations in which a friend practices the serve while you practice your returns. Work hard on the return; if you have a dependable return of serve, it will increase the pressure on your opponent's serve, take some pressure off your serve and ultimately contribute to your arsenal of tennis weapons!

APPROACH SHOTS

An approach shot is any shot utilized to facilitate a player's gaining the net position. It could be a serve, a groundstroke, a volley or even a lob. An approach shot is really just what its name says it is—the hitting of a shot in such a way that you can approach the net behind it. It is not supposed to be an outright point winner, but it is supposed to put your opponent on the defensive while permitting you to gain an offensive position.

Thus, an approach shot should have the following characteristics: *hit deep* into the backcourt to force your opponent to return from behind the baseline; *hit to an opponent's stroke weakness,* usually the backhand, or to where an opponent is weak by position; *hit with underspin* since this causes the ball to "float" (remember, shots hit with backspin tend to rise in flight) through the air, thus giving you more time to move in to the net—underspin also causes the ball to skid to a low bounce, thus forcing your opponent to hit up; *hit with medium speed,* since the harder you hit, the sooner the ball comes back and medium speed coupled with depth gives you time to move in to good position. Most intermediate players get their first taste of approaching the net behind a groundstroke; the following section will deal with that situation. Later on, you will want to develop your ability to approach the net with other shots (i.e., serve and lob) as well.

You have an opportunity to go to the net when your opponent hits short and the ball lands in the vicinity of your sevice line. You can tell approximately where the ball will bounce by noting its speed and trajectory as it leaves your opponent's racket; low, net skimming shots do not usually land deep in the court, thus they give you a good opening. If you can hit from inside your baseline, you should take advantage of this opportunity to go to the net.

1. Move forward into a good position (try to hit on the rise, no later than at the top of the bounce) and stop—get set—to hit your shot. As you increase in skill, you may wish to learn a running approach shot, but for now, remember that "hit-and-run" is illegal!

2. Stop; turn your side to the net; use a short, compact, high-to-low swing; keep a firm wrist at contact; and follow through.
3. Move on forward instantly after contact, following the ball to the net, moving forward toward the side of the center line to which you have hit your approach shot. If you have hit a forehand down the line to your opponent's backhand, you should attempt to reach a net position three or four feet to the right of the center line. Such a position bisects the angle (see chapter 5) of your opponent's possible return.
4. Just as your opponent's racket makes contact with the ball, you should come to a "split-step" stop, both feet set apart as in your ready position; once you determine the direction of your opponent's return, move into position to make your next shot. Again "hit-and-run" is undesirable—running wildly through your first volley will produce many more errors than necessary.

THE LOB

When your opponent rushes the net, your play is a drive down the line, a short crosscourt shot or a lob. The lob can keep the net rusher honest and may be a significant factor, as it has been on many occasions, in the outcome of the match. It can be used against the player who crowds the net and who depends on the serve and volley to win matches. The lob, especially an offensive lob, forces this player back to the baseline into a weaker position. The lob, usually a defensive lob, also provides valuable time for the player drawn out of position by an opponent's placement. Don't underestimate the value of the lob. Learn it well, and use it!

The lob is started the same way as the groundstrokes, whether on the forehand or backhand side. Grip, stance, and backswing are identical; the tournament player uses this initial movement to disguise an offensive lob and thus wins many points outright. When returning one of your opponents' hard-hit shots, the backswing may need to be more abbreviated than usual. The difference between executing the drive and the lob lies in the angle of the racket face (the "eyes" look up) as contact is made with the ball, in the exaggeration of the low-to-high path followed by the racket as it moves through the forward swing, and in the distinct *follow-through* required to hit a satisfactory lob. Lobs may be hit with either topspin or backspin; they demand all of the timing and precision of the other strokes, possibly a little more.

Two types of lobs are generally identified—the offensive and the defensive (fig. 3.2). The offensive lob is hit either flat or with topspin just over the opponent's reach to a target area in the backcourt. In doubles, it is mixed up with crosscourt returns to keep the net player from moving too far and too often from a normal net position. The flat lob is difficult to control and is not used as much as the topspin; topspin lends an element of control and at the same time causes the ball to jump away from the opponent after the bounce. Remember that the offensive lob is most effective when well-disguised, so do not give away your intentions. Practice it as though you were hitting a high topspin groundstroke and mix it up with your normal groundstroke practice. Use the following reminders: get your feet and body set into a good groundstroking position; start the racket

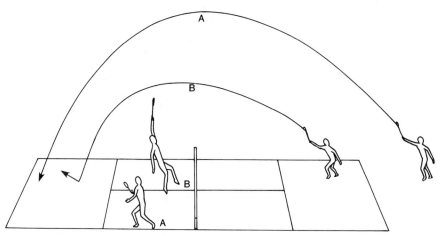

FIGURE 3.2 Offensive and defensive lobs. The defensive lob (A) is used to help a player get out of trouble; usually hit from deep in the court, it has a high trajectory and is aimed at a target deep in the opponent's backcourt to give you time to recover your position. The offensive lob (B) is used as a surprise tactic and is usually hit from inside the baseline with a lower trajectory that just clears the extended reach of your opponent, landing in the middle of the backcourt.

head below the ball; stroke from low to high; "brush" up on the backside of the ball; and finish with a high follow-through.

The defensive lob is used primarily when you have been forced out of position by an attacking shot and you need *time* to recover for the next shot. It is usually hit with some degree of underspin, which causes the ball to slow down and hang in the air. A good defensive lob has a much higher trajectory than an offensive lob and should be hit to a target area just inside the baseline. When lobbing defensively, remember the length of the court from baseline to baseline and hit the ball to go the distance. Defensive lob reminders include: get your feet and body set into good groundstroking position whenever possible (you may not always have time to do this!); start the racket head below the ball; lift the ball up and forward; finish with a high follow-through.

Learn to lob offensively and defensively with both the forehand and backhand. A beginner frequently attempts to drive the ball past an opponent, even when hopelessly out of position. This aversion to the lob and to other "dink" shots usually gives the opponent the edge at the net. With experience, players soon realize the importance of the lob and use it more often.

THE OVERHEAD OR SMASH

The answer to the lob is the overhead or smash. It is one of the most vital shots in tennis. Lack of a good overhead will defeat a net attack, while ability to smash will provide the weapon to finish off many rallies. After the overhead has been perfected, it provides a real sense of satisfaction and accomplishment.

Ready Position

Turn

Sight

Contact

Finish

FIGURE 3.3 The overhead smash

The overhead stroke, in many ways, is similar to the serve. The main differences are that the ball is "tossed up" by the opponent—not the smasher—and the player *must move* to get into position to hit the ball. It is not a simple shot to make because of the careful positioning and precise timing required to hit the ball well. As in the serve, the ability to direct the ball to specific targets is as important as the ability to smash with good speed.

There are two basic overhead shots, the smash at the net and the smash from the baseline after the ball has bounced, usually the result of a high, defensive lob. Both are important and time must be taken to learn each one well.

The grip is basically the same as that used for the serve. When played close to the net, the ball is hit fairly flat. Like the groundstrokes, early preparation is essential in hitting a good overhead. As soon as you determine the return is a lob, *turn your body sideways* to the net and begin moving your racket into position. Most of the time you will turn, step back with your right foot, and *slide* back under the lob, keeping the ball in front of your body. If the lob is very deep, you may have to turn and run back. In each case, you should reach a position behind the ball and alongside its flight path. Finish with your weight on the right foot so that it will be easier for you to transfer your weight forward and into the shot. Simplify the motion of your backswing by bringing your racket up in front of you (rather than swinging it down past the foot as in the serving backswing) and then taking it back behind your head. The motion takes place as you begin your turn away from the net. Pointing at the ball with your left hand may help you keep your eye on the ball as well as making certain it remains in front of you. Prior to hitting the ball, drop the racket head behind your back, then move into the hitting zone by rotating your shoulders forward, extending the arm and snapping the racket head through the ball. The ball is hit about one foot in front of the right shoulder and as high as possible with a flat racket face. After contact, continue your follow-through, the same as you would for a hard, flat serve. Finish with your right foot swinging forward to maintain your balance, take a step forward, and then recover quickly to your position at the net. Direction is controlled by the use of the arm and wrist, the racket head being made to close forward and downward at the moment of impact. The angle of the racket face varies according to the distance from the net—sharper when close, more open as you move back.

A deep lob to be returned after the ball has bounced may be played as a smash or as a groundstroke. As soon as you spot the high lob, run as quickly as you can to a position well behind where you expect the ball to bounce. Judge the bounce by "reading" the spin applied by your opponent and prepare for the return as you did for the short lob. In order to smash, the rebound must be high enough to be hit as an overhead. Hit the ball back deep, with spin (usually slice), to keep your opponent back. If your opponent has come to the net, you have the option of returning a lob of your own.

You may not always be able to hit the ball with both feet on the ground. Sometimes the ball is lobbed just high enough so that you have to jump to make the smash. When this happens, push off your right foot as you move your racket up in front of you; leap up and land on your left foot (scissors kick). Make certain you snap the racket head firmly through the ball, and then quickly recover for the next shot.

DROP SHOTS AND DROP VOLLEYS

Drop shots and drop volleys are the whipped cream of a player's game and are very definite complements to the all-around game. They require a very delicate control or "touch" and must be well-timed and well-disguised to be successful.

The drop shot is used to draw a baseline player in to the net, to move a slow player who has been caught deep in the backcourt, or to wear down an opponent with a drop shot followed by a lob. It is a very delicate shot and is usually attempted when the player is in a good offensive position, well inside the baseline. The closer you are to the net, the more effective the shot will be; since the ball travels a shorter distance, your opponent has less time to reach it.

The drop shot is executed after the ball has bounced; it is hit with underspin, gently, with a *relatively level* trajectory, so that it just clears the net and lands *short* in the opponent's forecourt. *Deception* is critical to the success of this shot, so your preparation and stroke must look as normal as possible until the very last second. In order to disguise your intentions, take a backswing similar to that of your normal slice groundstroke. Step into your shot, swinging your racket forward from high to low. The ball is hit to the side and in front of the body with a relaxed wrist. Just before contact, open the racket face to brush the back and underside of the ball, thus imparting backspin to the ball and slowing down its forward motion. The follow-through continues downward and forward; keep the ball on the strings as long as possible; recover to an alert ready position immediately! If your drop shot is too deep, you're in trouble; a good drop shot will bounce at least three times before leaving the service court. See if you can do it!

Take a central position well forward of the baseline for practice of drop shot returns of balls delivered to you by a ball machine or a partner. Can you stroke the ball so that it bounces at least 3 times in the opponent's service court? Keep score to see whether in 20 tries you are successful as many as 8 times, 12 times, 15 times, 18 to 20 times. Ask a partner to judge whether you are disguising your intent to hit the drop shots.

A drop volley is used only when the player is at the net; like the drop shot, it is a surprise shot and should not be overutilized. The drop volley is hit with underspin so that it barely clears the net and lands short in the opponent's forecourt. Your preparation and backswing should be similar to that for your normal volley. Move the racket head downward and forward, opening the racket face slightly to brush the underside of the ball, so that at the finish, it is almost completely open; at contact, relax the wrist and let the racket head "give" slightly, thus deadening the impact of the ball on the strings, causing the ball to lose some of its speed, and producing a very short volley. The follow-through is short, since you must recover quickly in case your opponent can get to the ball. Angle the ball away from your opponent whenever possible. A good rule to follow is not to use the drop volley if the ball can be put away with a deeper volley.

Reminders for the drop shot and drop volley are: use normal preparation in order to disguise your intentions; watch the ball and concentrate on your shot (above all, *do not* look at the intended target); swing forward and downward— gently; make contact on the back and underside of the ball with an open racket face; follow through naturally for the drop shot; use a shorter follow-through for the drop volley.

Practice the drop shot along with your groundstrokes, and your drop volley along with your volleys. Mix them in with your normal strokes, learn to disguise them, and you will add two more weapons to your arsenal!

HALF VOLLEY

The half volley is neither a volley nor a groundstroke, but rather a defensive shot hit on the rise (fig. 2.5) immediately after the bounce. It has often been compared to the dropkick in football. There will be many occasions when you will be trapped as you move to the net and do not have time to get into position for a forcing volley or cannot volley at all. You have already covered several yards of court space, consequently you must adjust your stroke by keeping both backswing and follow-through to a minimum. Actually, you place your racket behind the ball so the ball meets the racket instead of the racket moving forward to meet the ball. The speed of the ball as it rebounds from the court surface provides the power for the return. The point of impact is in front of the player.

The shot is controlled by the angle of the racket face, and this increases in importance as you move closer to the net. The face is opened as you approach the net to raise the ball. However, when you half-volley from the backcourt, the face is closed to prevent the ball from rising too high on the return. With practice, you will learn to adjust your racket to attain the proper trajectory.

FOOTWORK AND TIMING

Good footwork and timing are the trademarks of the finished player. How often have you watched an athletic contest and thought to yourself, "My, how easy they make it look!" This ease of execution comes only after hours of hard work—work on the basic strokes and work on the means of getting into the best position to execute them with as near perfect weight control and balance as possible. And timing, which some people are fortunate to be born with, can be learned so well that it becomes automatic. You can incorporate these attributes into your game by practicing the footwork suggestions made in Chapter 2, by using the practice drills described in the next chapter, and by applying the suggestions on tactics found in Chapter 5. Eventually, you too will make it look easy.

4 Progress Can Be Speeded Up

There are many ways to speed your progress, only a few of which are presented here. Of course, one of the best is to play frequently against all kinds of competition. However, *playing* tennis does not always provide enough practice to improve your specific weaknesses nor to further develop your strengths; thus, some form of concentrated practice on specific aspects of performance will probably be beneficial in improving your game.

Before you continue, it is important for you to understand that practice does not make perfect unless your practice is purposeful. Repeating a stroke or drill over and over again without being aware of the reason for it or without using it correctly may cause you to *re*gress rather than *pro*gress. So, be sure that you *practice with a PURPOSE.*

GENERAL CONDITIONING AND WARM-UP

Tennis is a strenuous game when played competitively, and it requires a certain amount of conditioning. Conditioning includes proper diet, adequate rest periods, and a good mental attitude, as well as exercises designed to develop stamina, agility, flexibility, strength, neuromuscular coordination, and speed.

How can you prepare yourself for competitive play? First, you must understand what conditioning involves. You can train alone, which is more difficult and not much fun, or you can train as a member of a class or team under the guidance of a teacher, coach or trainer. In any case, training involves three general areas: warm-up, conditioning, and stretching and strengthening. These must be made part of your daily regimen and adhered to consistently. Exercises that approximate the demands of actual competition in which vigorous effort is interspersed with brief opportunities for rest (that is, between points and while changing ends) meet the criterion of specificity. This criterion, which is an important principle in improving performance, demands that the exercises utilized in a conditioning program be specifically related to, and impose stresses similar to, those of the activity for which the conditioning is being done.

Warm-up is the key to injury prevention as well as preparing you to begin your play at full stride and efficiency from the very first point. Warm-up must be *purposeful* and *planned*. Just "hitting" with someone is not enough. Warm-up is designed to get you going, to loosen muscles, and get the blood circulating to all parts of the body. It raises body temperature, and when drills are used, warm-up calls upon "muscle memory" to prepare for hitting the ball. In order to obtain these benefits, warm-up should be aerobic, with increased heart rate, for at least two minutes.

Warm-up is intended to get you ready to play, not tire you out. Too much warm-up may cause you to fade in the final set of match play. Especially in tournament competition, where on-court warm-up is frequently limited to five minutes, much of your warm-up should be done off the court so that you can use available court time for your stroking practice. Easy jogging, stretching, and calisthenics are examples of warm-up activities that can be done off the court. All tournament players should warm up sufficiently before going onto the court. Prematch stretching is essential. Keep in mind that proper warm-up can win the first two or three games. If you are a slow starter, or if the temperature is cool, warm-up is tremendously important.

Design your own sequence of off-court warm-up activities (including stretching, calisthenics, and easy jogging or slow rope jumping) that are vigorous enough to induce a feeling of complete readiness for your on-court stroke practice, but do not cause you to use energy that will be needed in actual play.

Stretching and strengthening exercises are included in your conditioning. Stretching is your key to injury prevention, prevention of stiffness, and ability to relax. It must be done *before* and *after* practice to avoid stiffness and to relax the body. After practice, or a match, it is important to cool off properly. The key areas to stretch are the neck, shoulders, spine, inside and front of the thighs, groin, hamstrings, calves, and Achilles tendons. Stretching is done smoothly and slowly without bouncing; hold the stretch position between 15 to 30 seconds. Never force a position, but allow for gradual movement to the end of your range of motion. Avoid extreme deep knee bends, crouches, or bouncing in this position in order to prevent injury to the knees. Also, avoid straight leg sit-ups and double leg raises while lying on your back. Use bent knee sit-ups with the knees bent at least 90 degrees; these should be done on a padded surface or on the grass, not hard-surface tennis courts.

Distance running is recommended to develop circulorespiratory endurance (aerobic conditioning); wind sprints—walking 30 steps, jogging 30 steps, sprinting 30 steps and then repeating—(anaerobic conditioning) are recommended to develop speed and leg strength. Forward and backward running, including sudden stops and starts, quick changes in direction, sliding, running up and down stairs, as well as running in place at various tempos are all good conditioning activities. Rope skipping is another popular warm-up and coordination exercise which you may use to supplement running. The following are also recommended:

1. Squeeze a tennis or sponge ball to develop the muscles used in gripping the racket.
2. Do push-ups and sit-ups to develop arm, shoulder girdle and abdominal strength.
3. Practice stroking with the cover on the racket.

Remember, these exercises do not take the place of hitting tennis balls, but they should not be neglected. Use prudence and discrimination in the amount of time you spend on each, but include some type of specific exercise in your schedule. As you become a more finished player, you will need to increase the work load in order to further improve strength, stamina, reaction time, and overall coordination.

PRACTICE DRILLS WITH RACKET AND BALL

This section provides exercises and drills to help you master tennis skills. Some are for beginners, others for intermediate players, and still others are quite advanced. Most of the drills include suggestions for making the practice situation progressively more difficult. Some of these you can practice alone, some with a partner, and others with members of your class, team or other group. Always keep the following concept in mind—practice makes perfect when the practice is purposeful, is done in good form, and achieves the desired results.

Holding your racket with the "choked grip" (the hand near the throat of the racket), can you tap the ball to the ground so it will bounce approximately waist-high 50 times in succession? Keep your left foot in place. Can you tap the ball into the air 50 times without allowing it to fall to the ground? Practice the flip drill keeping the ball in play by tapping it into the air with alternate sides of the racket face. See how many taps you can get in one minute.

Shorter periods of time during which real practice occurs will be much more effective than longer periods of time spent in half-hearted effort. Just as overloading is an important principle in developing strength and endurance, so is overlearning an important principle in developing skills. *Thousands* of balls must be hit *correctly* before the skills will become automatic. Concentrate! Work hard! Soon you will find your game developing into the type you had hoped for.

Without a Partner

Backboard Rally   From distances of 15, 25, and 30 feet, stroke a ball against the backboard using the basic groundstrokes. Add the net line to the backboard and resume practice. Play the ball on any bounce at first, concentrating on form and hitting it correctly. Later, when correct stroking form is habitual, play the ball on one bounce, hustle into position, and concentrate on footwork.

Serving Practice   When serving form has become consistent and correct, place a hula hoop or a tennis ball container on one of the desirable aim points (identified in the self-evaluation question p. 76) and practice hitting your serve to a specified aim point. Move the target to several of the desirable aim points and practice in both service courts. Be sure to maintain correct form while practicing. Do not sacrifice speed and spin in order to gain accuracy.

How many times can you repeatedly rally a ball against a backboard?

Volley Practice   Stand approximately ten feet from the backboard, and practice volleying a ball against it. Spend the last five minutes of each practice session volleying with the cover on the racket.

Stroke Developer Practice   If you have a stroke developer (ball suspended on elastic shock cord, fig. 4.1), use it whenever you can to groove your groundstrokes, serve, and volley. Strive for perfection.

Tethered (Rebound) Ball   Stroke the tethered ball (fig. 4.1) across the net and keep it in play either on the forehand or backhand side at first, then alternating forehand and backhand strokes.

With a Partner

When you have a partner to work with, your practice drills can be more fun, especially if you inject the element of competition. At the same time, you will be able to help one another by making corrections and suggestions.

Partner Drop-and-Hit   From the side-to-net position, stroke balls, dropped by your partner, across the net and deep into the opposite court. You and your partner should be standing behind one baseline about three feet away from each other, and your partner should *drop* the ball at the perfect point of impact for your swing. Select target areas for placement practice. When hitting to backcourt targets, the ball should clear the net by three or four feet.

FIGURE 4.1 Tethered ball, serving ball, and stroke developer

Toss-and-Hit across the Net This drill is similar to the drop-and-hit drill except that you start in the ready position and the ball is *tossed* to you instead of dropped. Vary the practice by having your partner toss long and short balls, some right at you, others away from you.

Rally Practice Using the service court lines as boundaries, keep the ball in play by hitting it back and forth across the net. Start each rally with a self-drop-and-hit. Later, move behind the baselines, and use the regulation court. Play the ball on any bounce at first—concentrate on form and on hitting it correctly. Later, when correct stroking form is habitual, play the ball on one bounce, hustle into position, and concentrate on footwork.

Deep-Court Game Draw lines approximately nine feet inside of and parallel to both baselines. Play a set, using a baseline game—Rushing the net is against the rules of this game!—counting every ball falling short of the nine-foot line as an "out" ball. Later, follow "short" balls in toward the net, and attempt to volley.

Placement Drill Beginning with a self-drop-and-hit, stroke the ball across the net attempting to hit it to your partner's forehand. Keep the rally going, attempting to hit every ball to the forehand. Later, practice placing all your shots to the backhand. Both players should return to the center of the baseline after each hit. Be sure to reverse roles so that your partner can practice placements, too! As your skill increases, add difficulty by combining the deep-court game with placement practice. With three players, A hitting against B and C, player A hits crosscourt shots while players B and C hit down-the-line shots. Players rotate clockwise at specified intervals.

Serve and Return of Serve Serve to both right and left service courts to your partner who will return the serve. Alternate staying back and advancing to the net after each serve. The receiver attempts to return balls deep when you stay back and attempts to play the return short and low when you rush the net. Do not attempt to volley the return at first—concentrate on the serve and the return. You may volley and play out the point later.

Volley Practice From a good volleying position at the net, volley balls that have been stroked to you from the baseline. At first, have your practice partner hit only to your forehand side, then only to your backhand. Then be prepared to volley shots hit in any direction—to your forehand or backhand, right at you, high or low. Rotate roles so your partner can practice the volley too. When volleying, concentrate on keeping both the backswing and forward swing as short as possible.

With three players, player A volleying from a *net* position against players B and C stationed behind the baseline, player A aims each volley alternately to the deep corners. Since there are two players behind the baseline, player A can volley aggressively, while players B and C try to get every volley after *one bounce,* and return shots designed to make player A stretch and scramble. Rotate to all three positions.

With two players standing near their respective service lines on opposite sides of the net, volley against your partner. Try to keep the ball in play at first, and then volley low toward the feet to provide practice on those more difficult low volleys. Finally, try to volley past each other.

Lob-and-Smash Practice   One or two players start in a good net position and smash against two players lobbing from behind the baseline. Exchange positions at intervals. While the lobbers should concentrate on retrieving every smash, the smashers should hustle into good position under each lob and work on meeting the ball squarely, as high as possible, and out in front.

There are many other fine practice drills which might be used. In addition, you can devise practice situations to suit your own needs. Practice situations should be gamelike, should demand correct performance of skills, and should place increasing stress on the player. Whatever the situation, remember that the way you perform the skills while practicing is what counts. Fundamentals build sound foundations, so don't count on luck, depend on skill!

THE GRADUATED LENGTH METHOD

A very popular and successful method of learning the basic tennis skills is the one known as the GLM or "graduated length method." It is similar to that used by many ski instructors in which students start with short skis and gradually progress to the full-length ones. In most cases, students are able to experience early success which in turn motivates them and keeps them from experiencing frustration. For the student having difficulty in learning to contol the full-sized racket, the GLM may be the answer.

The GLM is based on the theory that an individual is able to control and to adjust more quickly to activity in the area immediately in front of and close to the body. As the distance between the body and the end of the lever increases, some learners experience more difficulty in controlling and adjusting their movements. It is important to understand that the movements of the hand, arm, feet, and the rest of the body utilized in stroking are similar, regardless of whether the student is holding or simulating holding a racket. Holding the racket at the face, the throat, the shaft, or just above the leather changes the length of the lever. Shortening the lever reduces the tension on the wrist and makes for better control. Because of this, the stroking pattern is more easily and quickly learned. Graduation to the full grip and stroke progresses smoothly.

The following presentation is a condensed version of the GLM, not an indepth analysis. For the student experiencing difficulty in controlling the full-size racket in the beginning, this could provide the means of making a satisfactory adjustment. For the advanced player having difficulty with stroke production, "going back to basics" may be a means of overcoming this problem. Two directions may be taken in the "simplified approach." GLM progressions may take place by starting with the hand, moving to the paddle, then the short racket and finally, the full-size racket. Another way to utilize a GLM progression is to start with the hand, then hold the full-size racket at the face, then at the throat, at the shaft, and finally at the regular grip. Because most students have a full-size racket, the latter procedure will be described here.

The Groundstrokes

The analysis of the stroking pattern for the forehand and backhand drives is the same as that described earlier in the book (Chapter 2) except that the racket is not used until the desired stroke pattern is mastered, using only the hand (fig. 4.2). Following is a suggested progression.

Ready Position   **Turn**

Step   **Contact**   **Finish**

FIGURE 4.2 GLM—Using the hand

Hand Progression   Before beginning your stroking pattern with the hand, it is important to understand the comparison between the hand and racket. The fingers of your hand correspond to the strings; the hand and wrist to the throat and shaft of the racket. Tighten the strings by keeping the fingers straight. Straightening the fingers will also tend to straighten the wrist.

Practice the same stroking pattern suggested in Chapter 2, i.e., *Ready, Turn, Step, Swing, and Return,* without the racket (see fig. 4.2). The ready position is taken with the right hand either closed (as though holding a racket) or with the hand open, the fingers extended. The hand remains closed until the beginning of the forward swing and may either remain open through the stroke or close again after moving through the impact point. Going through the stroking patterns without the racket will make it possible for you to practice your tennis strokes almost anywhere, i.e., your living room, yard, lawn, etc. For the backhand, the extended thumb may be used as the "face of the racket."

When you have mastered the stroking patterns, the following hand-ball exercises will help you to become familiar with ball control and develop your hand-eye coordination.

1. Ball bounce drills
   a. With the fingers extended and wrist firm, bounce the ball down to the court, keeping it in play. Walk around, bouncing the ball under control. Then bounce the ball upward off the palm of the hand.
   b. With the hand in the vertical position, bounce the ball with the bottom edge of your hand.
2. Stroking drills from a self-toss and from the side-to-net (stroking) position.
   a. Toss the ball slightly upward in the direction of the right net post so that it will bounce opposite your left foot. When the ball has reached the top of the bounce (about waist-height), swing the right hand forward and catch the back side of the ball. Hold at that point and check your contact point.
   b. Toss the ball up, catch it and continue your follow-through and finish.
3. Stroking drills from a self-toss and from the ready position.
   a. Repeat 2a and 2b except that the movement is initiated from the ready position.
   b. Remember: *Turn, Step, Swing!* Make your toss after you have completed your turn.

Note: Backhand toss-and-catch and backhand toss-and-hit are not practical and are omitted at this time.

4. Repeat the exercises in 2 and 3 except that instead of catching the ball, stroke it to a partner or against a wall. Keep your hand in the semi-vertical position throughout the stroke, contacting the ball with the palm of the hand. Hold your finish and check your position. Stroke the ball only a short distance (12–15 ft.) to avoid hurting your hand.
5. Repeat exercise 4; except that you will now hit a ball tossed to you by a partner. A few practice tosses may be necessary to get the ball to bounce softly and start to come down opposite the left foot (a "friendly toss").

6. Repeat exercise 5 except that the ball is tossed away, long, short and directly to you. Practice moving to get into good position to make your "stroke."

Racket Progression   Once you have mastered the hand exercises, practice with the racket will move along rather smoothly. The progressions are the same except that now you will be hitting the ball with the hand on various parts of the racket. The acceleration of the racket head through the ball will vary depending on the distance you wish to hit the ball. The amount of time you spend on each phase will be governed by your own ability and learning speed. In some instances you may wish to speed your progress by eliminating a step or two. It might also be necessary to go back a step to reinforce your stroking patterns.

The progression on the racket begins with the racket being held with the hand at the throat of the racket and the fingers on the strings (see fig. 4.3). One, two, or three fingers may be used. This will place the palm of the hand on the same plane as the face of the racket. On the backhand, the knuckle of the index finger is placed on top of the throat and the thumb diagonally up the throat (see fig. 4.4). In the forehand side-to-net position, care must be taken to keep the butt of the racket in front of the right hip, pointing toward the net. In the backhand, the right thumb is in front of the left hip and under the arm. Practice self-toss-and-hit drills and hitting tossed balls from both sides (forehand and backhand), and then alternate hitting forehands and backhands to your partner. (See figure 4.5a, b.)

From the strings, the hand is moved to the throat of the racket (see fig. 4.6) and then just above the leather grip (see fig. 4.7). As the hand moves down the grip, the distance between tosser and hitter increases, as does the acceleration of the racket head through the ball. From the grip above the leather to the full grip, the ball is stroked across the net (until then, a court is unnecessary) (see fig. 4.8). At first, the balls are hit back from a few feet behind the service line, then from behind the baseline. Following toss-and-hit exercises, rallying begins,

FIGURE 4.3 GLM—Forehand grip, fingers on the strings

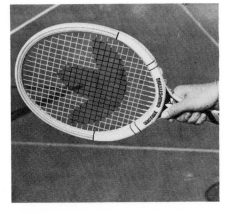

FIGURE 4.4 GLM—Backhand grip, thumb at the throat

FIGURE 4.5a GLM—Self-drop-and-hit to partner

FIGURE 4.5b GLM—Partner toss-and-hit

first without a net, then softly over the net, and finally baseline to baseline. Begin your rally by tapping the ball up to yourself once or twice, allowing it to bounce each time, and then stroking it softly to your partner. Start lifting the ball across the alley lines; then from sideline to sideline, and finally across the net. When you have gained racket and ball control, stroke the ball without stopping it. If you are not in good position, stop the ball with your racket and then stroke it back across the net. Begin with your hand just above the grip and work down to the full grip. When you have gained control and become consistent, practice rallying crosscourt, forehand to forehand, then backhand to backhand. Practice crosscourt rallies, then keep one ball in play by four players. Complete your rally progression with three players on the court keeping the ball in play. Practice placement by trying not to hit the ball back to the player who hit to you last. Using the tap-up-and-hit, both short court and full court will make it possible for you to sustain a longer rally, and also to practice good footwork and stroking patterns.

FIGURE 4.6 GLM—Backhand, at the throat

FIGURE 4.7 GLM—Forehand grip, above the leather grip

Forehand

Backhand

FIGURE 4.8 GLM—Toss-and-hit
across the net

The Serve

Like the groundstroke, the serve may be learned with a paddle and short racket, or with the normal tennis racket. This presentation will disregard the paddle and short racket.

The basic serving motion is similar to that of throwing a ball overhand, so practice begins throwing a ball overhand to a partner or against a wall. The left foot is placed at a forty-five-degree angle, right foot parallel, the feet comfortably spread. An arrow through the toes should point in the direction of the intended serve. The left foot is kept in place during the throw. The wrist and elbow are kept loose, with the wrist rotated so that the back of the hand is toward your face at the finish. Next, the ball toss as described earlier is practiced. Following is a suggested progression.

1. From the serving stance, without the racket, drop the right hand, lift it toward the back fence (knuckles up) to a position parallel to the ground, then bend the elbow allowing the hand to drop behind the back. This is the downward-upward swing. At the completion of the motion, toss the ball in the direction the left foot is pointing.
   a. Reach up and catch the ball, the right arm fully extended, the back of the hand toward your face.
   b. Repeat, except that the right arm and hand will extend toward your target area.
   c. Repeat, following through past your left side.
2. Repeat 1, except that the toss-and-catch motions are combined. Down together, up together and catch.
3. Repeat 1 and 2 except that instead of catching the ball, strike the ball with the inside of the extended fingers. The ball is hit to a partner—or to a wall. The distance between partners, or from the wall, is approximately 15 feet. Serve the ball into your partner's hands. Practice this motion until you can toss the ball and hit it accurately to your partner.

4. Take the ready position as described in Chapter 2 ("The Serve"). Move the right hand so that your grip is above the leather. From this position, repeat the moves suggested in exercise 3 of the hand progression discussed in this chapter. When working on the court with a partner, begin by "serving" the width of the court from sideline to sideline—down-up, toss, and hit. When you can do this successfully, serve across the net from the service line. Gradually work your way back to the baseline. (Your partner may practice the return of serve by stroking the ball softly back to you.)

5. Complete the progression by holding the racket by the grip and serving from the baseline into the appropriate service courts.

(**Note:** If you have difficulty with the full swing, start with the racket in the position it would be prior to the forward-upward motion into the ball, i.e., the elbow shoulder high and bent, the racket behind the back. Toss-hit!)

The Volley

The GLM progression for volleying is similar to those described for the groundstrokes and serve. Begin with the hand and gradually work from the strings of the racket to the grip. Like the groundstrokes, forehand and backhand volleys are learned simultaneously. The instruction, like the groundstrokes, is based on a tosser and volleyer working together. In this progression, one partner tosses a ball underhand (a "friendly" toss) directly to the appropriate target. By tossing correctly, the tosser forces the learner to use the crossover step, to shift the weight forward, and to execute the task with proper mechanics.

1. From the side-to-net position, the feet together, the hand up with the back of the hand toward the face, step forward and catch a ball tossed to your hand from a distance of 15 feet. Step-Catch.

2. Repeat the toss-and-catch, except that the movement is initiated from the *ready position.* Turn-Step-Catch.

3. From the ready position, turn, step and "volley" the ball back to your partner with the extended fingers. Turn-Step-Volley.

Note: Like the backhand groundstroke, the volley practice at this time is limited to footwork and "hitting with the thumb."

4. From the ready position, the fingers on the strings: turn, step, and volley the ball to your partner's hands. For backhand volley practice, take the backhand grip with the thumb diagonally across the throat of the racket. Volley the ball, first from the side-to-net position, then, from the ready position. When you have mastered both volleys, alternate hitting forehands and backhands from the ready position.

5. Move the grip just below the racket throat and repeat the previous exercises of number 4. As the grip moves down the shaft, the distance between partners is increased but the volleyer must volley gently enough (by easing the grip) so that the tosser can catch the volley. Concentrate on keeping both your backswing and forward swing as short as possible.

6. From the ready position at the net, the volleyer, using the regular grip on the racket, volleys balls tossed across the net. The tosses are varied, some to the forehand, some to the backhand, some high, some low, etc. Tosses to the center of the body are played with the backhand; at the face, with the forehand. Watch the ball and be prepared to change the angle of the racket face (closed for high balls, open for low ones).
7. From the ready position at the net, volley balls that have been stroked to you, first from in front of the baseline, then from behind it. Volley deep, clearing the service court.
8. With one person at the baseline and one at the net (one up, one back), keep the ball in play with groundstrokes and volleys.

In utilizing any of the suggested GLM progressions, patience cannot be overly stressed. Take time to master each phrase of the progression before going onto the next. As the hand moves down the shaft of the racket, it becomes apparent that the stroke through the ball must be made with more authority. The stroke becomes longer, the transference of weight more pronounced. Practice the patterns! Have patience! Transition from hand to full grips will take place naturally—and "painlessly!"

5 Patterns of Play

Specific rules of strategy for every possible situation cannot be established. There are, however, general principles that all players can apply to their own games. In addition, there are common situations which every player is likely to encounter during competitive play; these include serving, returning the serve, playing in the backcourt and playing at the net. This chapter will present general principles of strategy and some specific applications of the principles to the common playing situations.

Skill in stroking is not the only requirement for a winning game. Players must utilize brain power and must apply their intelligence to the situation at hand. Consideration should be given to the *conditions of play,* including wind, sun, and court surface; it is essential to *understand your own psychological makeup* so that you can emphasize, develop, and apply positive personality characteristics; and you must *analyze your opponent,* including both psychological and physical characteristics in your analysis. Once you realize that the thinking player has an advantage, you will have taken a very large step forward in improving your performance. That tennis is a game requiring skill cannot be denied, but *inability to use the available skill most effectively is often the cause of a losing game.*

PSYCHOLOGICAL CHARACTERISTICS

In addition to skill and intelligence, your psychological characteristics have an important influence on your performance. Spirit, a will to win, a determination to overcome adversity, poise under pressure, respect for yourself and your opponent, confidence in your abilities, and a healthy attitude toward competition are all positive psychological attributes which can enhance your participation in tennis. Players who focus only on winning or the fear of losing will miss the *JOY OF PLAYING*! Tennis is a game, not a life or death situation; it provides many opportunities for personal growth, improved skills and increased confidence. It can be played with great intensity and with tremendous concentration; but the focus should be on your own performance, *doing the best that YOU can do.* Doing your best requires that you control your emotions so that you can stay calm, think clearly, make necessary adjustments in strokes or strategy, and *enjoy* the effort. Success should be measured in terms of your own improvement; the winning and losing will take care of itself. One famous coach had standard words of advice for players going out to play a match: "Watch the ball, move your feet, concentrate, and have fun!" "And have fun" were the most important.

PRINCIPLES OF STRATEGY

Following is a discussion of nine general principles which can assist you in playing a more intelligent game.

1. **Play through your strengths to your opponent's weaknesses.** Weaknesses may be inherent stroke weaknesses, or they may be created by moving your opponent out of position (see principle 5). A common stroke weakness of many players is the backhand, but individual players may have other weaknesses as well. Learn to recognize these and strive to exploit them. The warm-up period just prior to a match provides an excellent beginning for these obervations, but remember to keep alert throughout the match. If your opponent likes hard drives, hit soft-angled balls with a variety of spin; if a player has a good net game, keep the ball deep and use an astute mixture of passing shots and lobs; if a player does not like to play net, use a combination of drop shots followed by low drives, thus forcing a difficult volley. Be careful about playing the weakness too often, since obviously, an intelligent player will try to protect it. Hit an occasional shot to the forehand, thus making the next shot to the backhand more difficult to handle. A player may improve a weakness during match play because an opponent continually plays to it, thus providing the practice that is evidently needed! Save the shot to the weakness until you really need a point, when you're behind 15–40 or when you finally get the advantage in a long deuce game (see principle 7). Note that your opponent's strongest stroke may not be the steadiest.

As you warm up on the court, do you make a systematic effort to feed your opponent a variety of shots and placements so that you can detect strengths and weaknesses? Do you then incorporate your knowledge of these strengths and weaknesses into your game strategy?

Remember, also, that you must plan your strategy around the shots which you can execute successfully, especially those that you can hit consistently even under the stress of match play. As Vic Braden says, "Hit the shots you *'own'* "! If you do not have a good net game, it is pure folly to charge the net at every opportunity just because you think it is the way to beat a particular opponent. Instead, stay in the backcourt and play the shots you can hit effectively. *Plan your strategy around your strengths.*

Try to neutralize your opponent's strengths through the intelligent planning of overall strategy, alert observation of opponent patterns of play, and concentration on playing the best you can in your match, not the one on the next court!

After the match, as you continue to practice, *work to develop the shots you needed*; learning to play an all-court game and enlarging the arsenal of tennis weapons that you can use with confidence, gives you the valuable advantage of flexibility in future matches.

2. **Bisect the angle of your opponent's possible returns.** This is a basic theory of position play which says that as soon as you hit the ball, you *immediately* place yourself in the best possible position to defend your court. DON'T WAIT to see whether your shot will be in; if you do, you won't be ready for the next shot. AND DON'T STAND THERE ADMIRING YOUR SHOT, for while you're

doing that, your opponent may be hitting the ball back past you. The ready position you know about already. The best court position is usually in the *middle* of the return *angle* available to your opponent, not necessarily in the middle of the court. This angle will change with every shot you hit, thus the direction of your shot is an important factor in determining your position.

Consult Figure 5.1a. If your opponent is returning the ball from point X, the two dashed lines going from X to the corners of the singles court identify the return angle available. Your best defensive position is in the middle of that angle, somewhere along the dotted line. Note that when you hit down the middle, your defensive position is in the middle of the court.

The next diagram (fig. 5.1b) illustrates the angle available to a player hitting from point Y. Your best defensive position is bisecting the angle somewhere along the dotted line. If you are in the backcourt, you should be slightly to the right of the center mark; if you're at the net, note that your position should be to the *left* of the center service line.

The next diagram (fig. 5.1c) illustrates what can happen if your opponent returns from point Z. Again your best defensive position is along the dotted line, bisecting the angle of possible return. In the backcourt, you'll be to the left of the center mark; in the forecourt, to the right of the center service line.

If your opponent has drawn you wide of the court to the spot marked YOU (fig. 5.1d), your choice of return will influence how far you have to move in order to bisect the angle. If you hit down the line toward point Z, you'll have to move two or three steps further to get into a good defensive position; but if you hit crosscourt to point Y, you'll be much closer to bisecting the angle of your opponent's possible return.

Consider this principle as you select your shot; and as soon as you make your shot, assume a good defensive position, bisecting the angle of return.

3. Keep the ball in play. Concentrate on steadiness, accuracy, and consistency. Make your opponent hit the ball. Do not try to make your shots too good. Give yourself a margin of safety; let your opponent try to "thread the needle." Concentrate on hitting *each shot* over the net and within the court boundaries. Give your opponent one more chance to make an error.

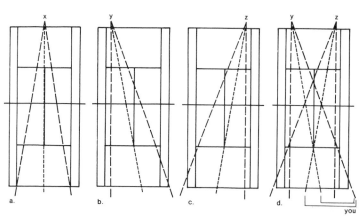

FIGURE 5.1 Bisecting the angle

4. Keep your shots deep—and your opponent behind the baseline. A deep shot is one that lands near the baseline, thus forcing your opponent back and on the defensive. Let your opponent be the first to hit a short ball. One very basic principle of tennis strategy is "down the middle and deep" (fig. 5.1a). This reduces the size of the angle into which your opponent can hit, thus giving you less court to cover (fig. 5.2); it gives you more time to prepare for the return, since the deeper your shot, the greater the distance your opponent's shot will have to travel; and it prevents, or at least makes it more dangerous, for your opponent to advance to a more aggressive net position.

In order to hit your shots deeper, you may need to focus on hitting the ball higher. Generally speaking, net-skimmers land near the service line; shots with higher trajectories, clearing the net by four or five feet, generally land near the baseline; not only will the depth of such a shot be to your advantage, but in addition, the higher bounce of the shot will force your opponent either to play a difficult shoulder-high return or to retreat even further behind the baseline. When both you and your opponent are playing from the backcourt, keep your shots *deep* with *medium height* and *medium speed*.

5. Keep your opponent moving. Make your opponent *run*—from one side to the other, up and then back, from one short angle to a long, deep angle. Never let a player get set. This principle is related to principle 1, since in applying it, you are trying to maneuver a player out of position, thus creating a position weakness from which the player cannot cover the open court.

Many players may be able to run from side to side quite well, but there are few people who can run up and back and still make effective returns. A crosscourt shot hit into the deep corner, followed by a down-the-line shot into the short corner and another shot to a deep corner (in fig. 5.3, successive shots hit to targets

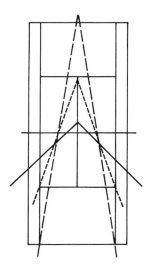

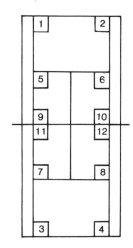

FIGURE 5.2 Keeping the ball deep reduces the area into which your opponent can return.

FIGURE 5.3 Shot placement targets: 1, 2, 3 and 4 are deep corners; 5, 6, 7 and 8 are short corners; 9, 10, 11 and 12 are drop-shot targets.

1, 6 and 2) can be a more effective sequence than merely hitting first one deep corner and then the other deep corner (in fig. 5.3, moving your opponent back and forth between targets 1 and 2). Although there is some danger in hitting short shots, the risk may be necessary in order to lure your opponent into a weak position or to force a player into hitting on the run. The effective combination of drop shots followed by lobs is a very difficult one to beat. And when you finally do manuever a player out of position, don't become overanxious or excited trying to blast a winner into the opening or you may hit it over the fence! Just watch the ball (not your opponent), get into a good stroking position (don't be lazy), and *concentrate* on hitting the shot well.

6. **Change the pace.** Keep your opponent off balance and guessing all the time. Vary the speed, the spin, and the placement of your shots. Hit one ball hard and deep, the next one deep but softer, the third one angled short with topspin, and the fourth one deep with backspin. If you have established a shot sequence of hitting alternately to the deep corners, upset your opponent's anticipation by hitting two shots to the same corner. Changing the pace is a good antidote if your opponent has applied principle 5 to you; as you scramble to chase down shots hit to various locations, slow things down by changing the pace, keeping the ball soft and deep.

7. **Play percentage tennis.** There are several aspects to this principle which basically advises a player to hit "safe" shots, that is, shots that will be effective 80 to 90 percent of the time.

First, remember that more points are "lost" on errors than "won" on placements. Review principle 3; avoid careless errors; don't try high-risk shots that are unlikely to be successful; master new shots in practice to the extent that you can hit them consistently and confidently before trying them out under the stress of match play conditions.

Second, note that more errors are made by hitting into the net than by hitting long. So raise your sights and hit those backcourt targets.

Third, if your opponent has moved you out of position, your best choice of return is a long crosscourt drive rather than a drive down the line. The net is lower in the center than at the sidelines, and the court is longer, by approximately five feet, from one corner to the deep corner *diagonally* opposite than from the same corner to the deep corner *directly* opposite (fig. 5.4). Thus your *margin of error is greater on the crosscourt,* and since this shot travels the longer distance, it also gives you more time to recover your position. Look again at Figure 5.1d and note that when you hit crosscourt, you don't have to move as far to gain a good defensive position, bisecting the angle.

Fourth, be aware of the score. Know which points and which games are crucial. Actually, every point and every game are important, but certain points are more critical than others. On these critical points, you should play percentage tennis by avoiding careless errors and utilizing appropriate shot selection.

Try to win the first point in each game; it can help you to gain a psychological edge. The fourth point is also critical; if the score is 15–30 and you win the point, you are even, but if you lose the point you are rather far behind; if a player is ahead 40–15, that player has two chances to win the game. Other crucial points occur at 40–30, 30–40, ad in and ad out, since only one point is needed to win what must have been a very close game.

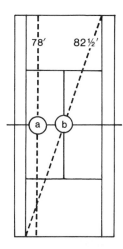

FIGURE 5.4 Court dimensions down the line: = 78 feet; crosscourt = 82.5 feet. Net height at the sideline (a) = 3.5 feet, net height in the middle (b) = 3 feet.

Another way to get a jump on your opponent is to win the first game in each set. In the beginning of the match, be sure that you have warmed up properly *prior* to getting onto the court; *be prepared* to go all out the moment the match starts; an early lead may force your opponent to change tactics and will certainly increase the psychological pressures. If you win the first set, don't let up at the start of the second set; keep the pressure on and don't give your opponent a chance to get started. If you lose the first set, work especially hard on the first few games of the second set and you may catch your opponent coasting. Once the momentum has shifted in your favor, keep it going (see principle 9)!

In singles, when both you and your opponent are in the backcourt, if your return lands near the baseline and beside the opponent's right alley, should your ready position be to the left or right of the center mark in order to "bisect the angle"?

Many strategists feel that the seventh game of each set is very important; if the score is 4–2 and you win that game, you're decisively ahead at 5–2; but if you lose, it's 4–3 and your opponent has almost caught up.

Critical points and games are times for intelligent decisions, not increased tension or panic. Your calm recognition that a critical point is at hand should lead to the selection of appropriate high-percentage shots. Use less critical points and games to explore opponent weaknesses and play percentage tennis!

8. Anticipate. This is one of the best general rules, although admittedly quite difficult to use effectively. It is possible, however, so start developing this quality *right now! Where you hit the ball* governs the possibilities your opponent has in making the return (see principle 2). In addition, you must *analyze your opponent's pattern of play.* Is a deep forehand usually returned down the line or crosscourt? Where does your opponent usually return a backhand? Many players have great difficulty hitting a backhand down the line. (They're really just lazy and need to move their feet into the proper position!) If your opponent falls into this category, you can hit a deep shot to the backhand, advance to the net, and be waiting to volley away the customary crosscourt return.

Anticipation requires that you divert some of your attention away from the ball in order to *watch your opponent.* Notice *how* the ball is hit because the methods of stroke production will frequently reveal intent. For example, if the ball is contacted late, it will probably go down the line, but if it is hit early, it is most likely that it will go crosscourt. If the backswing is high, backspin will probably be imparted to the ball, but if the backswing is low, the ball will usually carry topspin. Note the location of the ball toss when your opponent serves (also the angle of the racket face), and you may be able to profit from your keen observation.

Can you recall several suggestions for gaining a psychological edge over your opponent? Do you make it a practice to use these tips?

Anticipation enables you to cover more court, get more balls back, get yourself in better position to hit the ball, and play a better game more easily. It is most discouraging to an opponent who thinks a ball has been put away, to see you move easily a few steps and return it effectively, just because you knew all along where the shot was going and got a head start in that direction.

9. Do not change a winning game—always change a losing game. If the strategy you decide upon is working well and you are winning, keep it up. Do not relax, let up, or start practicing some new and fancy shot. Your opponent may suddenly catch fire and you probably will not be able to return to your previous level of play.

However, if your opponent begins to utilize some effective strategy against you, then you must change your tactics. If you are losing, by all means, try something else. You have nothing further to lose by trying other tactics, and you might find the answer to your opponent's game.

A few words of caution are necessary for you to apply this principle correctly. Changing a losing game *does not* mean that you should change your stroking style; methods of stroke production should be mastered in practice. Obviously, if you're making errors in stroke production, i.e., taking too long a backswing, using improper footwork, not watching the ball, etc., these need to be corrected, and the sooner the better!

However, this principle refers to strategy, not stroke production; and to knowing *when* to make the change. *Don't panic* into changing too soon, just because your opponent made a lucky shot, or a great one (it may never happen again!), or because you are making errors. Correct the errors before changing strategy; and if correcting the errors does not seem to be within the realm of possibility on this particular day, then change the strategy. For example, if you decide on a net attack as your best strategy, don't retreat to the baseline the first time your opponent passes you. Give the strategy a fair chance. On the other hand, if you are being passed three out of four times throughout the first five or six games, maybe something else will be more effective, so don't wait too long to make the change.

COMMON PLAYING SITUATIONS

It's all very well to read about principles of strategy, but it is quite another matter to understand and to apply these principles to specific playing situations. This next section presents selected applications for four common playing situations: serving, returning the serve, playing in the backcourt, and playing at the net. To facilitate your understanding, both *singles* and *doubles* are discussed in each section. Commentary regarding position play and stance indicates appropriate position for the *beginning* of a point, not a static position to be held throughout the point. Positioning is *dynamic* and changes with every shot. Review again principles 2 (bisect the angle) and 8 (anticipate), then adjust your position on the court accordingly.

Serving

Stance   In *singles,* it is generally best to stand near the center mark to serve, although some players prefer to stand about three feet to the left of the center mark when serving to the left court, thus making it easier to serve to the receiver's backhand (principle 1). Note when you stand near the center mark to serve that immediately after the serve you are almost in the position from which you can best defend your own court against the return. If the serve is placed near the center line, the server has automatically "bisected the angle" (principle 2). Serving consistently from the same position will increase accuracy.

In *doubles,* the server's stance should be approximately in the center of the half of the court which the server must cover immediately after the serve. The server's partner is customarily stationed in a good net position, about eight to ten feet from the net, on the other half of the court, and as close to the center line as possible without jeopardizing the defense of the alley against a down-the-line service return. The server's partner takes this position on the assumption that the server will also come to a net position, preferably behind the serve, but if not then, as soon as possible thereafter (fig. 5.5).

Basic positioning for doubles teams demands that partners play *side by side* in a parallel relationship to each other (fig. 5.6a, b). The up-and-back formation is ineffective in covering the court since it leaves openings along both sidelines and also diagonally through the middle.

One variation of the customary doubles serving positions stations the server's partner at net on the same half of the court as the server and places the server as close as possible to the center mark (fig. 5.7). The server then approaches the net diagonally to cover the apparently open half of the court. This arrangement, sometimes known as the Australian doubles formation, locates the net player in perfect position to intercept the receiver's normal crosscourt return, forcing the receiver to adjust and perhaps to make a weak return. It may also be used to protect a server's stroke weakness. Suppose, for example, that the server has a weak backhand. When serving to the left court, the receiver's normal crosscourt return can attack that weak backhand; by utilizing the Aussie formation, the server's partner covers the crosscourt while the server approaches the net in position to utilize the stronger forehand stroke.

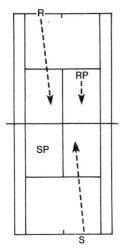

FIGURE 5.5 Letters identify the starting positions for both serving and receiving teams in doubles. Arrows indicate desired direction of movement for each player. The receiver's partner moves in only if the receiver makes a low crosscourt return or a good lob over the head of the server's partner.

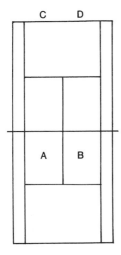

FIGURE 5.6a Play parallel: both partners up (A and B) or both partners back (C and D)

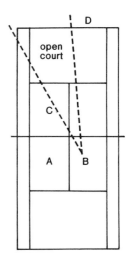

FIGURE 5.6b Disadvantages of one-up-one-back positioning: if C and D choose to play one up and one back, A and B will be able to hit through them into the open court; C becomes a "sitting duck."

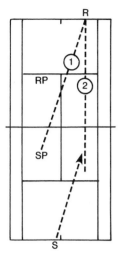

FIGURE 5.7 Australian doubles: (1) path of receiver's usual crosscourt return; (2) path of receiver's adjusted down-the-line return, which server can play with a forehand. This return creates openings for the serving team as in figure 5.6b.

Placement   Usually, the serve should be deep to either corner of the service court and should force opponents to return the ball with their weakest stroke, in most cases the backhand. However, occasional serves to the strong side will prevent covering up the weakness and will keep your opponent from getting set and grooving the return. Some serves should be delivered directly at the receiver's body, and the pace and spin of the serves should be varied (principle 6). The most common mistake in service strategy is a fireball first service (along with a prayer to help it go in!), and then, if the first serve misses (it almost always does!), a slow, dinky second serve—one any self-respecting receiver would hit away for a winner. Players would do better to develop a reliable first serve with medium pace and spin, together with a second serve only slightly slower and with slightly more spin than the first ball.

When playing doubles, which combination of letters represents the best positions for both players? A–B? C–D? E–F? Why?
What shots might be used to attack a team in position A–B? C–D? E–F?

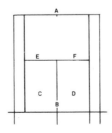

Which of the numbered targets are the most desirable aim points for your first service in singles? Why? In doubles? Why?

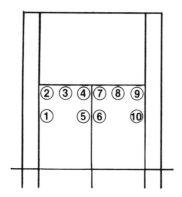

In *doubles,* the slower, spinning, and higher bouncing twist or topspin serve is usually advocated, thereby giving the server more time to advance to the net immediately after the serve. The flat serve hit with great speed is not too effective as a means of getting to the net because the return usually goes flying past the onrushing server before more than two or three steps are taken into the court.

Returning the Serve

This is one of the most important aspects of tennis. The position for receiving the serve will, of course, depend upon the type of serve your opponent is using. In *singles,* if it is a fast or high-bouncing serve, it is best to stand back of the baseline and just inside the imaginary continuation of the singles sideline. For slower or lower bouncing balls, one or two steps forward is a more aggressive position. The return of service should employ as many of the suggested principles of strategy as possible, but in many cases, particularly if your opponent has a good first serve, it is better to concentrate simply on getting the ball back. If your opponent has a very fast serve, you will probably not have time to stroke the ball with a full-swing groundstroke. Instead, attempt to block the ball back, merely letting the ball rebound from your racket, and concentrate on controlling the direction of your return. The return should be as deep as possible (unless the server is rushing the net) and away from the server, preferably to the weak side. If your opponent has a weak second serve, *step in* and take the advantage away with an aggressive and forcing return. Don't try for an outright winner unless you have an easy return. Hit as forcefully as you can without error. Use less force if you have to, but *keep the ball in play.*

In *doubles,* the receiver stands near the baseline and the singles sideline, and the receiver's partner stands in the middle of the other half of the court just inside the service line (fig. 5.5). If your opponent serves and immediately rushes the net, you should try to return the serve crosscourt to the server's feet, somewhere near the service line. This type of return will force the onrushing server to make a low and rather difficult volley or half volley. If you are successful in returning crosscourt, both you and your partner move up into a good net position, but if the return is weak or to the serving team's net player, the receiver's partner retreats to the baseline. The starting position of the receiver's partner is intermediary between offense and defense, and should be adjusted one way or the other depending upon the receiver's return. If the server's partner anticipates your customary crosscourt return and begins to poach effectively, you might try driving a return down the line behind the crossing net player or lobbing the return over the net player's head.

These are the three basic choices that the receiver has when returning a serve; skillful variation of the pattern can be a most effective strategy. If your skills are not yet quite up to this net-rushing style of play, both partners of the receiving team should play back behind the baseline in order to maintain parallel positioning (fig. 5.6).

Playing in the Backcourt

Against Another Baseline Player   In *singles,* this may happen often. The two opponents stay near the baseline and try to "outsteady" each other, each player making innumerable trips from one sideline to the other and each point finally being decided after the ball has made thirty or forty trips from one end of the court to the other. If patience and stamina are factors in your favor, this strategy may work for you. However, it is usually much more interesting to apply some of the principles mentioned previously. Try to pull your opponent up to the net with a drop shot, and then lob to force a retreat to the baseline. Keep your own shots deep (principal 4), and, if your opponent hits a short shot to you, utilize this opportunity to attack by moving in to hit it on the rise.

Against a Net Rusher   This situation occurs often in *doubles* when one team is on the offense in command of the net and the other team is forced into defensive play at the baseline. There are only three choices for the baseline players. *First,* they can lob over the heads of the net players and thereby dislodge them from the net. The primary danger of this choice is lobbing too low or too short, thus giving the net players an opportunity to win the point with a smash. The *second* choice is to hit a passing shot for an outright winner. When trying this down either sideline, there is danger of attempting to make the shot too good, hitting slightly long or wide or into the net. One of the best targets for a passing shot is the center of the court. The net is lowest in the center, giving you a greater margin of safety (fig. 5.4), and your opponents may also become confused about who should cover center balls. (The player whose forehand is in the center generally covers.) The *third* choice is to hit a relatively soft and low shot so that the net players will be forced to volley up. Many strategists insist that the basic idea behind all shots in doubles is to force your opponents to volley up, thus enabling you to win the point by hitting down past their feet.

In *singles,* the choices are the same. A *good lob* should dislodge your opponent from the net position and should prevent crowding the net in the future, thus making your low shots more effective. *Passing shots* are probably used more often in singles than in doubles and have more possibility for success because the net player has more court to cover in singles. Remember that the net player will try to anticipate your return, so be sure to vary (principle 6) your passing shots to keep your opponent guessing. If you have been aiming most passing shots crosscourt, try one down the line, even if it puts you into a somewhat weaker defensive position.

Keep your passing shots low, aiming for the short corners (fig. 5.3); this is one time when net skimmers are necessary. Hitting for the deep corners causes the ball to have a higher trajectory and shots that fly four or five feet higher than the net are a net rusher's delight!

If you hit a shot which can be reached, do a little anticipating (principle 8) yourself, and try to get a head start in the probable direction of the volley. If you are a good guesser, you may be able to turn what should have been a winning volley for your opponent into a winning passing shot for you.

Whenever you play against a successful net rusher, do all you can to keep that player in the backcourt away from the net. Make the net rusher's advance to the net as hazardous as possible by keeping the ball deep to a weakness (principles 1 and 4). If your opponent does get an opportunity to come in, try to hit your next shot toward the net rusher's feet, thus forcing a difficult volley. If you do force your opponent to make this low volley, anticipate a weak and short return, and move in a couple of steps so that you will be in good position to hit a potential winner.

Playing at the Net

Against a Baseline Player   In *singles,* if you are hitting from *inside your own baseline,* you have a good opportunity to advance to the net. Try to hit your approach shot deep, thus forcing your opponent to hit from *behind the baseline* and preferably with a weakness. The approach shot should put your opponent on the defensive and should permit you to obtain a suitable position for protecting your own court, thus down the line is usually a better choice than crosscourt (see fig. 5.1c). The approach shot itself is not intended to be a winner, therefore, it is neither necessary nor advisable to hit with extreme power. Usually a medium-paced, well-placed shot is most desirable since the medium speed provides the time needed by the net rusher to move from the backcourt to the forecourt, and appropriate placement puts the opponent on the defensive (see chapter 3).

Get as far into the forecourt as possible to make your first volley, but wherever you are in the court, *stop moving forward and get set before you make the shot.* It is quite possible that you may not be in good enough position to make your first volley a winner. If not, try to volley the ball deep and as far away from your opponent as possible, with the hope that you will be able to improve your position for the next volley. If you have made a good approach shot, forcing your opponent to make a weak return, and if you have achieved good position, try to make your first volley crisp and decisive so that it will be a winner. If your opponent can get to your volley, be sure that you bisect the angle of possible return (fig. 5.1). There is some danger in hitting angled volleys unless they are outright winners, because if your opponent gets to the shot, there is an extremely wide angle into which passing shots can be hit. Probably, the best advice is to volley deep to the backcourt until you can force such a weak return that you can easily volley it on the angle for a put away.

In *doubles,* control of the net is the most important factor in strategy for winning doubles. The two net players must cooperate in dividing the area of possible return (principle 2). Usually, angled volleys will be useful both as outright winners and as shots designed to maneuver the team defending the backcourt out of position. Net players should always be aware of the choices available to baseline players and should learn to anticipate (principle 8) passing shots and lobs. When the baseline team succeeds in lobbing over the heads of the net team, both players should retreat to the backcourt in order to maintain their parallel formation.

At higher levels of play, generally each partner is responsible for lobs hit over that partner's head; this practice clearly designates responsibility and in addition, maintains sound court position for that team. However, sometimes it may be necessary for one player to "cover" for a partner who failed to anticipate or who anticipated incorrectly. Thus, if the ball has been lobbed over your head, as your partner moves diagonally back to cover the lob, you cross over to the side of the court left vacant by your partner (fig. 5.8a). If your partner can return with an overhead hit before the bounce, you can maintain your net position, assuming that your partner will come back up beside you. However, if the lob is hit deep into your backcourt and your partner must make the return after the ball has bounced, you should retreat diagonally to the backcourt, thus returning to a side-by-side position with your partner (fig. 5.8b).

The baseline team that has just done such a good job of dislodging the attackers from their offensive position at net by lobbing over their heads should seize this opportunity to attack the net themselves. In this case, their lob has all of the characteristics required of a good approach shot (see chapter 3)!

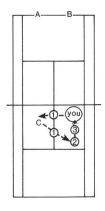

FIGURE 5.8a Covering the lob: as C moves diagonally back to cover, you move laterally left (1); after hitting the overhead (2), C moves up to a parallel net position (3).

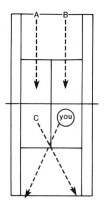

FIGURE 5.8b If the lob is deep to the backcourt: as C moves back to cover, you move diagonally back to the left side to maintain parallel position at the baseline. In this situation, A and B have an opportunity to move in to a good net position.

Against Another Net Player   In a *singles* match, it is relatively rare to find both players at the net simultaneously. Each player may utilize net play as a basic part of match strategy, but the point usually goes to the player who gets to the net first. Thus, the first serve is quite important since it is often strong enough to provide the server with the opportunity to advance to the net and control the play. It is foolish to rush the net if your opponent is already there, unless you have hit a shot requiring a difficult low volley and therefore anticipate a weak return or a drop volley.

In *doubles,* the four players are commonly found volleying away at the net. The key to success in this situation is to be ready, expecting every shot to come to you; be quick, using little or no backswing; and move in closer at each opportunity. This should keep your opponents back toward the service line, forcing them to play defensively while you and your partner play closer to the net to volley away their rising balls for winners. Remember that if the ball remains in play, you must adjust your position to accommodate your opponents' possible returns—and they could lob! So don't get too close!

SUMMARY

A winning game requires the following ingredients: *first,* skill and control of a variety of strokes; *second,* the knowledge of various patterns of play and the utilization of brain power; and *third,* appropriate psychological behavior, including the will to win. Regardless of your skill level, strategy and spirit can be important factors in determining the effectiveness of your performance. Even beginners can apply the principles up to the limitations imposed by skill.

You may have noticed that occasionally the principles offer contradictory advice. When your opponent's strength is steady baseline tennis, why keep the ball deep and play directly to that strength? Obviously, you'll need to size up the situation and follow the most appropriate combination of principles. While some players may prefer to *outhit* their opponents, there's a special joy in *outwitting* opponents! Try it—you'll like it!

les of the Game

The International Tennis Federation establishes rules, considers changes in and interpretations of the existing rules, determines the conditions under which international competition, such as Davis Cup and Federation Cup matches, takes place, and generally supervises the conduct of tennis throughout the world. The United States Tennis Association (formerly the United States Lawn Tennis Association) is a member of the ITF and thus conducts tennis programs in the United States in a manner consistent with ITF rules and policies.

While national and international competition is usually conducted in a highly technical manner (13 officials, including the umpire, a foot fault judge, and assorted line umpires are used to officiate one singles match between 2 players), the vast majority of tennis competition is conducted without any officials at all. Thus, it is extremely important for each player to assume the obligation to know and follow both the letter and the spirit of the rules. Actually, the official rules have remained unusually stable since the advent of so-called modern tennis in 1877. However, with the growth of professional tennis competiton and the development of open tennis, rule changes have been proposed and tried on an experimental basis, and some of the proposed changes have been adopted.

Rules are presented here in an informal manner and some illustrative examples are presented in an attempt to distinguish between the requirements of the rules and the traditions of long-established custom. Numbers in parentheses refer to the official USTA rule number.

Specifications pertaining to the court, it's permanent fixtures and equipment are contained in rules 1 through 4 (Chapter 1). The exact dimensions of the court are probably not too important to the beginner (or to the tournament player either). However, the names of the lines are another matter; they should become a part of every player's vocabulary. This knowledge is basic to an understanding of subsequent rules and to any discussion of strategy (fig. 1.1).

SINGLES

The Players and the Toss

In singles, the two players stand on opposite sides of the net. If you are the player who puts the ball into play, you are called the server and your opponent, the receiver. You serve for an entire game, and at the end of the game, you become the receiver and your opponent becomes the server. You and your opponent alternate serving a game and receiving a game throughout the match (5 and 15).

According to rule (6), contestants decide which one shall serve first and from which side of the net "by toss." The rule does not specify how this toss shall be made. Sometimes a coin is tossed. Frequently, one player places the head of a racket on the court and spins it like a top. Traditionally, before the spinning racket falls to the ground, the other player calls "rough" or "smooth." These terms refer to the knots in the strings: on one side the knots are "smooth" and on the other side, where the string has been cut off, the knots are "rough." Other means of identifying the two sides of the racket are also used—for example, "TAD or Davis" (printed on the top and bottom of the shaft); "M" or "W" or "right side up or upside down" (found on the end of the butt or side of the shaft). As the modern racket becomes more expensive, players are increasingly reluctant to let their costly rackets drop on a hard surface court; instead, they may choose to spin the racket while holding it loosely in one hand, stopping the spin by tightening the grip. However the toss is done, one player tosses and the other makes the appropriate call.

The player winning the toss may choose or require the opponent to choose from among the following: (1) to serve or to receive, and (2) to begin play on the north end or the south end of the court. The player not making the original choice has the choice of the remaining options. Note that if one player chooses the north end, the opponent is *not* automatically required to serve. Instead, the opponent has the remaining choice—to serve or to receive.

Usually, the player who wins the toss elects to serve first. Since many players consider the serve to be the most important offensive weapon, serving first provides not only a mechanical but a psychological advantage. Occasionally, however, a player may feel that it would be advantageous to receive in the first game, and will choose accordingly. The opponent, then, must serve the first game, and, in addition has the choice of end. As a beginner you may feel that your return of serve is stronger than your serve and, especially if the opponent's serve is rather weak, it may be to your advantage to receive first.

When the winner of the toss has chosen to serve first, the other player must be the receiver and must choose the end from which to receive. Usually, you should elect to receive on the "sunny" side of the court. This permits the server to serve the first game from the "shady" side, but, immediately after the first game when the players change ends and the receiver becomes the server, then you too will have the advantage of the sun at your back during your first service game. This well-established *tradition* in which the winner of the toss elects to serve and the receiver then "gives up the good side" leads many beginners (and indeed, many more experienced players as well) to believe erroneously that the winner of the toss gets both serve and side. Such is not the rule, nor is there any unwritten rule which says that the receiver must give the "good" side to the opponent. Strategy, not etiquette, determines the most appropriate choice. In fact, left-handed players have their own set of guidelines to go by and should study this rule carefully to gain what tactical advantage is available to them.

Delivering the Serve

The Position of the Server   The server must stand with both feet *behind* (*not on*) the baseline and within the imaginary extensions of the center mark and the singles sideline. When playing singles, the server may not stand behind the doubles alley. Essentially, the server's position is supposed to be a stationary one until after the racket has contacted the ball. Thus, the rules (7 and 8) specify that the server may not change location by walking or running, although slight movements of the feet during delivery are permissible.

Violation of the foot fault rule is probably the most common violation and one of the most annoying, especially in matches without an umpire. Even when an umpire is present, this rule is frequently not enforced, so that the responsibility for its observation rests almost totally on each individual player. The rule is very simple; the server is supposed to remain in a stationary position behind the baseline, not touching it at all with any part of the foot, until after the racket has contacted the ball. Note that the rear foot may swing over the baseline before the ball is struck, provided that it does not touch the baseline or the court. Immediately after contact, the server may put either one or both feet on or over the line into the court.

If you learn to perform the serve legally in the beginning, you will have no bad habits to break, and you will never be faced with the unnerving call of "Foot Fault!" on a crucial point, nor will you be faced with the arguments, accusations, and controversy that seem to surround players who serve illegally.

The Delivery Itself   Rule 7 states that the server, after assuming the previously described position, must toss the ball into the air and strike it before it hits the ground. The delivery is completed when the racket contacts the ball. Note that nothing is said about the manner in which the ball must be hit. Overhand, sidearm, or underhand motions are all legal (provided the ball is hit before it bounces) but, of course, the overhead pattern is by far the most effective.

Beginners (and even some advanced players), in preparing to serve, occasionally toss the ball very poorly. If you do not attempt to hit such a bad toss, it does not count against you, and you may toss the ball again (10). However, if you swing at the ball and miss, you have committed a fault. Since there is no penalty for *not* striking at a poorly tossed ball, the server should refrain from attempting to hit it. There is no limit to the number of times a player may toss the ball before it must be hit, although it is distracting to your opponent and a breach of etiquette if it happens too often.

Alternating Courts (9)   The server begins each game from the right of the center mark and serves to the diagonally opposite service court. The second point is started from the left of the center mark, and the server serves to the receiver's left service court, and so on, in alternating service courts until the game is finished. Whenever an even number of points has been played in a game, that is none, two, four, or any even number, the next point is started in the right court which is also sometimes called the even court. Whenever an uneven number of points has been played in a game, that is one, three, five, seven, or any odd number, the next point is started in the left court or the odd court.

Occasionally, a player will inadvertently serve from the wrong half of the court. If this should happen to you, remember that *all points played stand,* and you simply correct your position. In other words, the score stands but the inaccuracy of the server's station is corrected (9, 11).

Faults   On each point, the server has two chances to hit the ball over the net so that it will bounce within the boundaries (liners are good) of the diagonally opposite service court. A serve that is not good is called a *fault*. If the first serve is a fault, the server tries again, but if the second serve is also a fault, the server has committed a *double fault* and loses the point. The following list summarizes the ways in which a fault can occur (10).

1. The server commits a foot fault, either by assuming an illegal position or by touching the baseline before contacting the ball.
2. The server delivers the serve in an illegal manner.
3. The server misses the ball while attempting to strike it.
4. The served ball does not land within the proper service court.
5. The served ball touches a permanent fixture other than the net (such as a net post, the umpire's stand, the fence, the overhead lights) before it touches the ground.
6. In doubles, the served ball hits the server's partner or anything the partner wears or carries (39).

Let   The service is a let if it touches the top of the net and is otherwise good (14); that is, besides touching the net, it must be legally served, it must go over the net, and it must land within the proper service court (or on a line bounding that court). Note that a served ball which hits the net, goes over the net, and lands outside the proper service court—for example, in the alley, in the back-court, or in the other service court—is a fault. There is no limit to the number of lets that can occur. Any served ball meeting the above definition is a let and must be served over. The service is also a let if the receiver is not ready when the serve is delivered (14). Thus, the server should be sure that the receiver is in position before beginning to serve.

If a player is unable to play a shot because of circumstances beyond control, for instance, interference due to a ball from another court or to a spectator who suddenly moves into the way, that player may claim a let (13).

When a let is related only to a service, that one service is replayed. When a let is called to provide for an interruption of play, the entire point should be replayed. For example, if the first service is a fault and the ball is in play after the second serve, if play is *interrupted* by a ball from another court, upon resuming play, the server is entitled to two serves (13, 25).

Receiving the Serve

Although the position of the server must meet certain specifications, the receiver may stand in any position desired—on, in front of, or behind the baseline and on, inside of, or outside of the sideline or the center mark and their imaginary extensions (5). Strategy and skill, not rule, dictate the position of the receiver.

The receiver must allow the serve to bounce before attempting to return it, and the ball must be played before it bounces twice. The server wins the point if the receiver touches a served ball (other than a let) before the ball touches the ground (18).

The receiver must be ready when the serve is delivered. The server must wait until the receiver is ready for the second service as well as the first. If the receiver claims to be not ready and makes *no* attempt to return a service, the service is a let and that particular serve must be served again. If as the receiver, you attempt to return the ball, you may not then claim that you were not ready (12). However, the receiver should not stall or delay the play unnecessarily. You are entitled to clear the court of the first serve if that serve was a fault, but you are not supposed to distract the server unduly. The receiver must adjust to the reasonable pace of the server and be ready to receive when the server is ready to serve (30). Insofar as possible, the server is entitled to two serves in succession.

After the Serve

You lose the point if (20):

1. The ball bounces twice on your side of the net.
2. You fail to return the ball into your opponent's court.
3. You return a ball which hits a permanent fixture, such as the umpire's stand, *before it hits the ground.* However, if you hit a return that bounces within your opponent's court and then hits a permanent fixture, such as the side fence, *before your opponent can hit it,* then you win the point (23).
4. You touch the ball before it bounces, or volley it and fail to make a good return, even if you are standing outside of the court. This applies to the receiver who catches a serve before it bounces (18), or to the receiver's partner in doubles, who may be hit by a serve before the bounce, and in both instances, the receiver loses the point unless the serve is a let (39). Although the language is somewhat complex, the intent of the rules is clear and simple. You cannot call a ball out until after the ball has *touched the ground* outside the boundary lines of your court.
5. You deliberately hit the ball more than once in making a shot. The ball may not be deliberately carried or thrown off the racket. A double hit occurring in the course of a single, continuous stroke forward is legal, as are shots hit off the frame of the racket.
6. You, your racket, or your clothing touch any part of the net while the ball is in play.
7. You hit the ball before it crosses the net. However, you may contact the ball on your side of the net and permit your racket to follow through across the net, provided that you do not touch the net (24). The one exception to the rule against reaching over the net to hit the ball occurs if a ball in play bounces within the proper court on your side of the net and rebounds (because of the backspin placed on it) or is blown back over the net onto your opponent's side. In this case, you *must* touch the ball or you will lose the point, and you may, if you have to, reach over the net, without touching it, to do so (24).
8. You permit a ball in play to touch you, or anything you wear or carry, except your racket. Thus, if you run back under a high lob and the ball barely touches your clothing on its way down to the court, you lose the point.

9. You throw your racket at and hit the ball, even if you make a return that is otherwise good.
10. You *deliberately* commit any act that hinders your opponent in making a shot. If, however, the action that caused the interference was accidental, a let should be called and the point replayed (21, 25).

It is a good return if (24):

1. A ball lands on a boundary line, even on the outside edge of the line. The lines are considered to be part of the court which they identify, and a ball is not out unless it lands *completely outside* the line. In addition, an unwritten rule dictates that on any close ball, you give your opponent the benefit of the doubt (22).
2. The ball touches the net as it passes over, provided that it then lands in the proper court. Note that when this happens on a service, the serve is a let, but when it happens during a rally, the ball is in play.
3. The ball is returned outside the net posts *either above or below* the level of the top of the net, even if it touches the post, provided that it then bounces in the proper court.
4. A ball in play strikes a ball left lying on the court. The player must return the ball in play or lose the point. This particular situation could occur only through carelessness or laziness, since balls should not be left lying on the court. In championship play, ball retrievers clear stray balls before each serve is delivered. If you are acting as your own ball retriever, pick up all balls before each point is started, and, if the first serve is a fault, clear it quickly. Three balls are sufficient for a match, and extra balls should be left on the bench.

Scoring

Tennis has its own peculiar scoring system (26, 27, 28) which is quite different from those used in other sports. A contest or match in tennis is based on three units of scoring: points, games, and sets. A player must win at least four points to win a game, at least six games to win a set, and at least two sets to win the match. Thus, the minimum number of points in a match is 48, but in tennis, each point won by a player is called by its own name, not by the cumulative number of points that have been won. If you have no points, your score is called *love;* if you have one point, your score is *15;* if you have two points, your score is *30;* if you have three points, your score is *40;* and if you win the fourth point, you win the *game.*

   If each player has won three points, you would expect the score to be called 40–40 or 40 all, but such is not the case. This score is correctly called *deuce,* and one player must now win two consecutive points in order to win the game. The first point after deuce is called *advantage:* advantage in (ad in) if the server wins the point, or advantage out (ad out) if the receiver wins the point. If you have the *advantage* and you win the next point, you have won two consecutive points and you win the game, but if you lose the next point, the score is again called *deuce.*

Although the rules do not specify whose score is called first, the unwritten rules and the umpire's manual insist that the server's score is always called first. And indeed, to do otherwise and call the receiver's score first is grossly misleading. Most players will notice the considerable difference between 15–40 and 40–15!

To win a game, you must have won four points, and you must be at least two points ahead of your opponent. To win a set, you must have won six games and be at least two games ahead of your opponent. Thus, you have not won the set if the score is 6–5. If you win the next game, you win the set 7–5, but if you lose the next game and the score becomes 6 all, it looks like a long afternoon! (For an explanation of tiebreaker scoring rules, see page 90.) Fortunately, you don't have to be two sets ahead of your opponent to win the match. In a best of three sets match, you need to win just two sets—any two will do!

What is the score:

If the server has won	*And the receiver has won*
no points	*1 point*
2 points	*no points*
3 points	*1 point*
3 points	*2 points*
1 point	*1 point*
3 points	*3 points*
4 points	*3 points*
4 points	*4 points*
4 points	*5 points*
4 points	*6 points*

Most matches consist of two out of three sets, but in major championship tournaments, men's matches are usually three out of five sets. To win a best of five sets match, you must win three sets. The maximum number of sets in a match for men is five and for women three (28). This and the rule specifying rest periods (30) are the only rules that provide different conditions of play for men and women.

Changing Ends

Players change ends of the court after the first, third, and every subsequent odd game of *each set.* If the first set ends after an even number of games have been played (for example, 6–2), the players remain on the same end until after the first game of the second set. If the first set ends after an uneven number of games have been played (for example, 6–3), players change ends, play one game, and change ends again (16). This rule is intended to equalize adverse or advantageous playing conditions, such as sun, shade, wind, background, and the like.

Continuous Play

The rule states that "play shall be continuous from the first service until the match is concluded" (30). This rule is not a crucial one for the beginner. It applies primarily to tournament play, and its intent is to reward the player in the most fit condition. It permits a ten-minute rest after the third set (in a best of five sets match) or after the second set when women are competing. Tournaments utilizing tie-break procedures may eliminate the rest period providing advance notice is given. In the Boys' 18 division, matches are the best of three sets with no rest periods. In other junior divisions, matches are the best of three sets with an optional (at the option of any player) rest period in the Girls' 18 and Boys' 16 divisions. A ten-minute rest period before the third set is mandatory in all other junior events. Senior division (35 and over) matches are the best of three sets with an optional ten-minute rest prior to the third set.

When changing ends, no more than 1 minute, 30 seconds can elapse between the end of the game and the first serve of the next game. Stalling or resting between points, games, or when changing ends is supposed to be penalized, but the lengthy interpretation and explanation that always accompanies a statement of this rule illustrate both the complexity of the situation and the difficulties encountered in attempts to enforce it. A reasonable interpretation of the continuous play rule permits a player to sit down, towel off and have a drink during the regular changing ends process, but only within the 90-second time limit. The rule is, of course, completely unenforceable in a match played without an umpire. Since most players will rarely have an umpire, each player must assume responsibility for conscientious interpretation of the rule and for subsequent behavior.

A few comments might profitably be addressed to inexperienced or unsophisticated tournament players, especially to those who are on the way to a first tournament. Since "*play* shall be continuous," all warming up and practicing must be done prior to the *first serve of the match.* The social custom of permitting each player to take practice serves immediately prior to the first service game is in direct contradiction to this rule. Another social custom, that of permitting the server, before the first point of the first game served, to serve until a serve goes in ("first one in?!"), also disrupts continuous play. You may wish to make some adjustments of this rule in informal play, but don't let your feelings be hurt, and don't get into an argument if your opponent in a tournament match insists that all practice serves be taken before the match begins. Your opponent is absolutely right!

So that the play will not be delayed, time limits are imposed on the players' actions. What is the maximum time allowed between the end of a point and the next serve? How much time is allowed for changing ends?

In case of accidental injury, such as a sprained ankle or being hit with a ball or racket, a one time three-minute suspension of play is permitted, but play is never suspended to enable players to recover their breath or strength (30). Occasionally, a mishap involving a player's clothing may be interpreted as being due to circumstances beyond control, in which case a suspension of play to effect adjustment or repair may be permitted. To avoid misunderstandings, tournament players are advised to consult official USTA rules and the conditions of play specified on the entry blank of each tournament. This particular rule is an excellent example of one which is almost impossible to interpret according to its "letter" alone. However, the "spirit" of the rule is quite clear, and a good sport will abide by it.

DOUBLES

All of the above rules apply to doubles as well as singles, with the exceptions noted below (33).

The Court

The playing court for doubles is enlarged by the addition of the alleys. The service courts, however, are the same as those used for singles. Note that the server may now take a position behind the doubles alley if desired (34).

Serving in Doubles

The order of service is decided at the beginning of *each set,* and this order must be maintained throughout the set. Note, however, that the order of service may be changed at the beginning of any subsequent set. Teams must serve alternately throughout the match and partners must alternate serving for their team throughout the set (35). Thus, in a typical doubles match, if your team has won the toss and has chosen to serve, you and your partner decide which one of you will serve first. Usually, this decision is a tactical one, since most doubles teams want the strongest server to serve first. If your team decides to have you serve the first game, your partner must serve the third game. Your opponents must decide to have one partner, again usually the strongest server, serve the second game and the other partner must serve the fourth game.

This order in which each player serves every fourth game must be followed throughout the set. However, if you serve out of turn, your partner, who should have been serving, shall serve as soon as the mistake is discovered. All points or faults occurring before the discovery are counted. If a game is completed before the error is discovered, the service order remains as altered for that set (37).

As the server's partner, you may take any position on your side of the net, either in or out of the court. Thus, you may, in effect, obstruct the receiver's view of the serve, but note that if the served ball touches you, it is a fault (36, 39).

Receiving in Doubles

The order of receiving is decided at the beginning of *each set,* and this order must be maintained throughout the set, but it may be changed at the beginning of any subsequent set. In other words, partners must receive serves throughout the set on the same sides of the court. Thus, if in the first game, you receive in the right court, your partner must receive in the left court. In every game in which you are the receiving team, you both must be in your original positions (36).

The order of serving is *independent* of the order of receiving; that is, the first server for a team is not required to receive in the right court but may choose either side. Once you choose a side, you must receive on that side throughout the set (36).

If an error occurs and your team changes its order of receiving (for example, if your partner inadvertently receives a serve in the right court), the altered receiving order is maintained until the end of the game in which the error was discovered. You and your partner resume your original order of receiving in the next game of the set in which you are the receivers (38).

The receiver's partner also may take any position on the receiving side of the net, but note that if the served ball hits the partner before it bounces, the serving team wins the point (36, 39).

After the serve and its return by the specified receiver, the ball must be hit alternately by the opposing teams. Thus, either you or your partner, but not both of you, may hit the return into your opponents' court, in which case *either one* of the opponents may return it to your side. Occasionally, on a ball hit down the center between partners, both players will attempt to hit the return. Usually, one player gets there first and hits the ball while the other player hits the partner's racket. Since only one racket actually contacted the ball, this is a legal return (40).

TIEBREAKER PROCEDURES

Tiebreaking procedures have come into being in an attempt to reduce the length of tennis matches to a format more suitable for spectators and for television. Long-time tennis addicts will recall marathon matches that seemed to last forever, with set scores of 12–10, 16–14, 20–22, 8–10, and 17–15. Present-day fans can anticipate a conclusion within a much shorter time span. A tiebreaker goes into effect when the set score reaches 6 games all. During the past several years, several tiebreaking methods have been used: the 5 of 9 points "sudden death" method, the 7 of 12 points (the so-called Wimbledon) method, and the 7 of 13 points method used primarily by WCT. "Sudden death" is the term applied to the 9-point tiebreaker, since, if the score reaches 4 points all, whoever wins the next point wins the set and if it's the final set of the match (each player having won one set), that 9th point is match point for both players! In the 7 of 12 points tiebreaker, if the score is tied at 6 points all, play continues until one player is ahead by 2 points, thus minimizing to some degree a lucky shot, a bad bounce, or a fortunate net cord.

In 1974, the ITF decreed that the 7 of 12 points procedure is the only authorized tiebreaker; tournaments requiring ITF sanction must use that procedure, and in 1980, the USTA officially adopted the 12-point tiebreaker, requiring its usage in USTA sanctioned tournaments (27).

The 12 Point Tiebreaker

To win this tiebreaker, a player must win at least 7 points and establish a margin of 2 points. Score is kept numerically. When the score of the set reaches 6 games all, if it is your turn to serve, you serve the first point from the right court. Your opponent serves points 2 and 3 from the left court and right court respectively; you serve point 4 from the left court and point 5 from the right court. Your opponent serves point 6 from the left court. Players then change ends (no rest stop is permitted), and your opponent serves point 7 from the right court. If necessary, you serve points 8 and 9 from the left and right courts respectively, your opponent serves points 10 and 11 (left and right), and you serve point 12 (left). If points reach 6 all, players change ends and continue as before. You serve point 13 (right), your opponent serves points 14 and 15 (left and right). This pattern is followed until one player (hopefully you're the one!) goes ahead by two points, thus ending the set. The score of the set is recorded as 7 games to 6. Players change ends to start the next set; since you served first in the tiebreaker, your opponent serves first in the next set (fig. 6.1).

In doubles the same pattern is followed, with partners preserving their service order, but not necessarily serving from the same end from which they served during the set. For example, in a women's doubles match, Ann and Barbara are playing with Carlene and Doris (fig. 6.2). Ann and Carlene were the first servers for their respective teams. If the score of the set reaches 6 games all, it is Ann's turn to serve and she serves the first point from the right court. Carlene serves points 2 and 3 from the left court and right court respectively; Barbara then serves points 4 and 5 from the left and right court respectively; Doris serves the sixth point from the left court. The teams change ends and Doris serves the seventh point from the right court. If necessary, Ann serves point 8 from the left court and point 9 from the right court; Carlene serves point 10 from the left and point 11 from the right; Barbara serves point 12 (left). If points reach 6 all, the

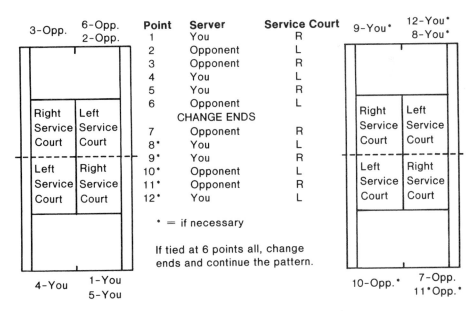

3-Opp.	6-Opp. 2-Opp.	Point	Server	Service Court	9-You*	12-You* 8-You*
		1	You	R		
		2	Opponent	L		
		3	Opponent	R		
		4	You	L		
		5	You	R		
Right Service Court	Left Service Court	6	Opponent CHANGE ENDS	L	Right Service Court	Left Service Court
Left Service Court	Right Service Court	7	Opponent	R	Left Service Court	Right Service Court
		8*	You	L		
		9*	You	R		
		10*	Opponent	L		
		11*	Opponent	R		
		12*	You	L		

* = if necessary

If tied at 6 points all, change ends and continue the pattern.

| 4-You | 1-You
5-You | | | | 10-Opp.* | 7-Opp.
11*Opp.* |

FIGURE 6.1 Tiebreaker procedures in singles

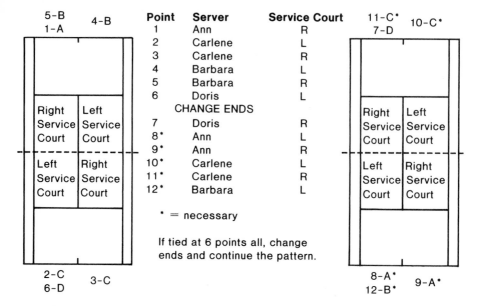

Point	Server	Service Court
1	Ann	R
2	Carlene	L
3	Carlene	R
4	Barbara	L
5	Barbara	R
6	Doris	L
	CHANGE ENDS	
7	Doris	R
8*	Ann	L
9*	Ann	R
10*	Carlene	L
11*	Carlene	R
12*	Barbara	L

* = necessary

If tied at 6 points all, change
ends and continue the pattern.

FIGURE 6.2 Tiebreaker procedures in
doubles. Ann and Barbara playing
against Carlene and Doris; Ann and
Carlene were the first servers for their
respective teams.

teams change ends and continue the same pattern. Barbara serves point 13 (right);
Doris, points 14 and 15 (left and right). The pattern is followed until one team
goes ahead by two points, thus ending the set. Teams change ends to start the
next set and since Ann served first in the tiebreaker, either Carlene or Doris serves
first in the next set.

Several procedural errors may occur in tie-break games, but only the most
common are dealt with here. When the score reaches 6 games all and players
erroneously begin an advantage game instead of a tie-break game, if the error
is discovered before the second point is started, the first point is counted and the
error corrected immediately. If the error is discovered after the second point is
started, an advantage set is continued until the score reaches 8 games all or a
higher even number; then the tie-break game is played. When an *error* is made
in the *order of service,* if only one point has been played, the point stands and
the service order is corrected immediately. When the error is discovered after the
second point is in progress, the service order remains as altered. In a doubles
tiebreaker, when a *partner receives out of turn,* if only one point has been played,
the point stands and the receiving order is corrected immediately. If the error is
discovered after the second point is in progress, the receiving order remains as
altered.

What are the advantages in the 7 of 12 points tiebreaker over traditional scoring and over the "sudden death" tiebreaker?

You can see that the 12-point tiebreaker is somewhat complicated, but it does avoid the "sudden death" problem and by requiring a two-point margin it is more like other aspects of tennis scoring; i.e., having to be two points ahead to win a game and two games ahead to win a set. In doubles, the 12-point procedure maintains the service order but forces players to serve from the ends of the court opposite the end where they have been serving during that set, and this happens at a crucial time in the match. Discussion of the pros and cons of various tie-breaking procedures continues, but tennis promoters, television producers and tournament directors strongly support scoring procedures which permit reasonably accurate estimates of the time that will be needed to complete a match. Undoubtedly some form of tiebreaking procedure will remain a part of tennis in the future.

"NO-AD" SCORING

A variation of traditional scoring procedures is the "no-ad" system, which is clearly defined by its name. A player must win only 4 points to win the game. Thus, if the score is tied at 3 points all (deuce according to the traditional system), it is game point for both players, since whoever wins the next point wins the game. On the seventh point, the receiver decides whether the serve will be made to the right or left court. Rather than love, 15, 30, 40 and game, the points are called zero, 1, 2, 3, game. No-ad scoring eliminates long deuce-ad, deuce-ad games, thus reducing the time required to complete matches. Many intercollegiate events are currently using this scoring system and it is very effective in physical education classes or other situations where time is limited.

7   The Unwritten Rules

Some unwritten rules of tennis have been mentioned in connection with other topics since they are woven into the fabric of the game. This chapter provides a brief summary of tennis etiquette. A small pamphlet titled "The Code" provides more complete guidance in these matters and is available from the USTA (see Appendix 3). Good manners are never out of place. They will help you to meet many tennis friends and to keep them.

Tennis has a tradition of sportsmanship—a tradition that can be exemplified by all players every time they step on a court. Many people feel that the Golden Rule, "Do unto others as you would have them do unto you," expresses the concept of sportsmanship clearly and simply. Others believe that a thorough understanding and application of the spirit as well as of the letter of the rules is the essence of sportsmanship. However you choose to define this ideal in general, there are specific attitudes and behaviors which characterize the tennis player and spectator who has both good etiquette and good sportsmanship. Practice them now and throughout your tennis career.

Player concentration is essential to top performance; thus, *no one* should do anything to distract either player. As a player, you do not make loud noises while the ball is in play and you avoid mannerisms or movements which may be distracting to your opponent. As a spectator, you should refrain from applauding, from talking, and from moving around until after a point or game is finished. *Quiet, please* is a basic tennis tradition that applies to everyone.

COURTESY TOWARD OTHER PLAYERS

Whenever you set out to play tennis, whether informally for fun and practice or in the more formal tournament and match-play situations, these characteristics will make you a desirable and knowledgeable competitor. You begin to develop them at home as you plan your tennis attire; appropriate clothing is a part of etiquette.

If you make a date to play, be there and be on time. It is particularly poor behavior to break a date or to default unless some real emergency occurs. It is even worse to break a date just because a better opponent happens to come along.

When walking to a court, proceed as quietly as possible outside the fence to the gate that is closest to the court to which you are going. Wait at the gate until the game in progress on the adjacent court is over, and then walk quickly past that court to your assigned court. *Never* walk onto a court where a point is in progress, even when playing in a social setting at your local school, club, or public park—always wait until the point is over. In tournament situations, wait until the game is over before crossing an occupied court, and then move fast. If in doubt, wait until the players change ends (you might even have to watch two full games) before you cross a court where a match is in progress. If a tournament match is going on and the only available court is adjacent to it, you should use that court only if your play does not disturb the match. If you wish to carry on a loud conversation with your friendly opponent from one baseline to the other, or if you are so unskillful that you cannot keep your balls on your court, and they continually interrupt the match, you should refrain from using that court until the match is over. You could, of course, use the court to play tennis without any conversation. Perhaps the added attention to your own performance would increase your control of the ball!

SHARING EXPENSES

Players should assume their fair share of the expense of the balls. Either offer to split the cost of new balls, or, if you play with one other person regularly, take turns bringing the new balls. If you agree to play with used balls, be sure that the ones you offer are in reasonably good condition.

GREETING YOUR OPPONENT

Before you play, greet your opponent in a friendly manner; introduce yourself to an unknown opponent. In a doubles situation, if two opponents know each other, they should take the initiative in introducing their partners to the others. The spin of the racket should be completed before going on the court to warm up. This enables the proper decisions to be made so that both players can warm up on the end on which they will play the first game. It is customary for the two players to check the height of the net at the center using two rackets (standard size rackets only), one standing lengthwise (27″) and the other sideways on top of the first one (9″), and to make the necessary adjustments, either in the tension of the net cord or the center strap (fig. 7.1). As you warm up, try to hit the ball to your opponent so that maximum practice is possible in the limited time available. This is not the match itself, and you're not supposed to be hitting winners or making your opponent run unnecessarily. All warm-ups should be completed before the match begins, and all practice serves should be taken by both players before any points are played.

SERVING AND RECEIVING

When you are the server, always begin a point with at least two balls in your hand or in your possession. Since play shall be continuous, it is poor behavior to start the point with one ball, serve a fault, spend the next few minutes chasing another ball, and then finally try to put the second serve in play.

FIGURE 7.1 Measuring the net. Use standard size rackets only (27" long, 9" wide).

Do you practice good tennis etiquette? Yes, you know what you should do, but what do you DO? Take the quiz titled "Do You Know the Score?" (pp. 147–148)

The server, according to rule, must wait until the receiver is ready for both the first and the second serve. Beginners, however, are sometimes unaware of this rule and, frequently when the first serve is a fault, will serve the second too quickly for the receiver to get set. If the first serve is a fault, the receiver is entitled to clear the ball from the court, so it will not interfere with the play of the point; this should be done as quickly as possible. Deliberate delay in clearing the serve is distracting to the server, and "quick serving" before the receiver is set is distracting to the receiver. Both acts are contrary to the rules and are breaches of etiquette as well. Also, consult the section on continuous play in Chapter 6.

KEEPING SCORE

Both players should keep score accurately, and the server should announce the point score (i.e., 15–30) before serving *each* point. Knowing the score is an important part of strategy and, in addition, prevents unpleasant disagreements. If a dispute regarding the score does arise, that is, you think the score is 15–40 and your opponent thinks it's 30 all, both of you should meet at the net (don't shout back and forth from one baseline to the other!) and try to reconstruct the points and the score verbally. If this process fails to reach an agreement, go back to the last score on which both sides do agree and resume play from there.

After each point, collect all balls on your side of the net and return them *directly* to the server, not just anywhere on the server's side of the net.

DISTRACTIONS—WHEN TO PLAY A LET

When one of your balls goes astray on an adjacent court, wait until the point in progress on that court is over and then say "Thank you for the ball, please." When a ball from an adjacent court comes onto your court, retrieve it promptly and return it directly to the player requesting it, or roll it gently to the backstop of that court. Some beginners are overly helpful and return a ball, say the first serve which was a fault, to the court from which it came while the players on that court are engrossed in playing out the point which is in progress from the second serve, thus actually interfering with the play. If a ball from another court enters your court in such a manner that your play was interfered with, ask your oponent to play a let. If you win the point and you're not sure whether something may have distracted your opponent, the courteous thing to do is to offer to play a let. If truly distracted, your opponent will accept your offer appreciatively, and if not, will say, "No thank you, it didn't bother me."

CALLING THE LINES

In situations in which there are no officials, you are responsible for officiating on your side of the net. This means that *you* call your own illegal shots such as double hits, touching the net, reaching over the net, double bounces, and the like. You trust your opponent to do likewise. It is a breach of etiquette to point your finger and say accusingly, "You touched the net, you touched the net!" *You,* not the spectators nor your opponent, are also responsible for calling, loudly and clearly, the lines on your side of the net. Tennis tradition demands that you give your opponent the benefit of any doubt. A ball hitting any part of the line bounding the proper court is good. If the ball is so close that a call is questionable, play the ball as good. There is nothing wrong with calling out balls "out"—even if they are close but wait until you see the ball definitely out before you call it. Note that the receiver, not the server, decides whether the serve is good. If the receiver makes no call and returns the ball, the server must be prepared to play it—the server cannot stand there and say, "But I thought the serve was out."

In general, if a ball is good, return it and *say nothing;* if a ball is out, call "out" and *do not* return it. *Never* make a call until after the ball has bounced. When a ball in play lands very close to a line, you must be prepared to return it if it is good. In fact, you *should* return it, and if you then see that it has bounced outside the proper court, call "out" *immediately.* Even though you have returned the ball, the bounce of the previous shot takes precedence, but only if you call immediately, *before* you see what happens to your return. Again, you trust your opponents to call the balls on their side of the net. Occasionally, on a sideline call only, you will be in the best position to make a call on your opponent's side of the net. If you are asked "How was it?", you call the ball as you saw it, even though you may have to call your own shot out. If your shot was out, you may call it out even if not asked—a good sport will do this. If you saw your shot good and you're not asked to make the call, you accept the decision, whatever it may be.

WHAT TO DO ABOUT QUESTIONABLE CALLS

Some people do not know the rules, let alone the unwritten rules; some people have never heard of "The Code;" some may not see well enough to make correct line calls; some players do make mistakes (we all do!); and, some people cheat, deliberately calling the lines and interpreting the rules in their favor. So what do YOU do about it?

First of all, you must be calm, cool and collected—advice that may be difficult to follow in the middle of a closely contested match. Secondly, make sure that *you* know the rules, and in addition, be certain that *your calls* are absolutely accurate. Your behavior and your attitude should be above reproach. Now, back to the problem! After the second or third questionable call made by your opponent, you could calmly ask, "Are you sure of that call?" This question alerts the player to your expressed concern that the lines are not being called accurately and may even improve the line calling. If your opponent expresses doubt about the call, a reminder that doubts should be resolved in your favor is in order. When your opponent insists that a disputed call is correct, you cannot change that call since you are responsible *only* for calls on your side of the net. While normally a player may not leave the court during a match, under these circumstances, you may go directly to the tournament desk to request an umpire. How much better if both players would call the lines properly, thus avoiding such unpleasant situations.

WHEN—AND WHEN NOT—TO TALK

Do not talk while the ball is in play. The one exception is in doubles when it is permissible for partners to call "yours" or "mine" to facilitate team play. Partners may also help each other in calling lines and you may call "out" or "bounce it" to aid your partner's judgment. Unnecessary conversation is not welcome between points either, since this distracts both players' attention. Of course, it is a nice gesture to compliment your opponent on good shots, but do not overdo it to the extent that either of you loses your concentration.

COACHING

Once a player steps out to play a match, coaching should not be accepted from anyone. From this time on, you are on your own, and this is part of the challenge of the game. There is no one to send in signals, to call the plays, or to analyze your opponent's weaknesses for you. It is up to you to figure these things out for yourself. Learn to be self-reliant; ask your friends, parents, and teachers to watch quietly, if they must watch, and to permit you to make and correct your own errors. During the ten-minute intermission, between the second and third sets for women and between the third and fourth sets for men, advice and discussion from friends or coaches is permissible since it does not interfere with continuous play. One exception to this rule (Rule 31) occurs during some international team competition when the team captain is seated near the umpire's stand and may converse with team members when the players change ends. Another exception may occur in interscholastic and intercollegiate competition, where by prior league or conference agreement, coaching may occur at specified times during the match, but only in such a fashion that does not interfere with the continuous play rule.

ATTITUDE

Your attitude is important. What you say and how you say it are the signposts others use in assessing you as a future partner, a friendly, congenial opponent, or a "let's not ask that one to be a fourth" type. Your opponent is not your enemy. You are both competitors, both wanting to play well, and both trying to raise your game to a high level. This is a joint venture, and there is no room for animosity. If you are not playing well, perhaps your opponent's good playing is the cause of your ineffectiveness. If so, issue a deserved compliment; your grumbling about your game is inappropriate and should not be foisted upon a respected competitor. Even if you are both playing badly, griping will not enhance the situation for either of you. Although it is probably impossible to play without some signs of emotion, temperamental outbursts are not considered good etiquette. Learn to control yourself, and you will be in a much better position to control the ball, your opponent, and the outcome of the match.

When playing doubles, it is not only poor etiquette, but it is also poor strategy, to criticize your partner. Obviously, your partner wants to play well; you do not help the situation through constant nagging. What is needed most is encouragement or perhaps a gentle reminder to watch the ball or to move your feet. Complaints about your partner's playing are not necessary. Concentrate on your own play, and perhaps your good shots will relieve some of the pressure or inspire better play. It is considered poor form to offer suggestions to your opponent, unless it is a practice match and a specific request has been made that you do so.

USING THE COURTS

Leave the court in a neat condition. Throw away empty ball cans, candy wrappers, and other debris into the nearest trash can, and do not leave trash or dirty towels cluttering the bench or the court.

When others are waiting, do not monopolize the courts. Most courts have rules governing their use posted on the fence or at the entrance. Know these rules and follow them. In some cases, players are permitted to play only one set of singles, but two sets of doubles. Sometimes players indicate that they are waiting for your court by placing a racket in the fence, which means that at the end of the set, you relinquish it graciously. Frequently, court rules limit the number of games played in a set to 13, so that when the score reaches 7–6, you relinquish the court, even though you haven't finished the set; or, when the score becomes 6 all, play a tiebreaker. It goes without saying that you never report the score incorrectly. Some courts are reserved for use by the hour, and when your hour is up, you should leave the court and not hold up other players who have reserved it for the next hour. If the courts are busy, it is your responsibility to share them equitably and according to local rule or custom.

Occasionally, you should offer to play or practice with players of lesser skill. This is particularly helpful to them, and you will be returning a favor that was done for you when you were not as skillful as you are now.

PLAYING IN TOURNAMENTS

For those of you who wish to experience the added challenges of tournament play, a few additional comments may be helpful. Study the rules and the unwritten rules carefully. Be sure you abide by both sets of guidelines. Read carefully the conditions of play which will be printed on the tournament's official entry blank. If you do not wish to abide by those conditions, do not enter that tournament. Entries should be filed on time and as directed by the entry blank, usually with entry fees enclosed.

When playing in a tournament, play your best. It is insulting to your opponent to offer anything less than your best effort, even if you are a much better player. To practice shots and "goof off" when playing a lesser skilled player is extremely bad manners. If *you* are the lesser skilled player, to quit trying, thereby offering no competition to your opponent, and playing less than your best is equally poor behavior. Treat your opponent with respect, and the favor will usually be returned.

If you are playing in a tournament where match and line umpires are present, make no line calls at all. Your responsibility is to play, and you return everything until you hear the call "out." The umpires assume the responsibility for calling the lines, and you should not dispute the calls. Line umpires do, of course, occasionally make mistakes, and sometimes an umpire will change a decision that was in error. If the call stands and it went against you, you accept it as part of the game. Occasionally, a player who knows that a line umpire's error resulted in a point that rightfully belongs to the opponent, will deliberately lose the next point in a gesture of sportmanship.

At the conclusion of a match, shake hands with and thank your opponent for the match. If you lost, offer congratulations to the victor and extend best wishes and good luck for the next round. Make no excuses for your play and recognize that your opponent was the better player. If you won, be a gracious winner, console your opponent about the loss and say something like "Good luck in your next tournament." As the winner, you should return all the balls to the tournament desk, report the score and find out when you are scheduled to play again; do this *as soon as possible* after the conclusion of your match so that another match can be assigned to the court without delay. When a chair umpire and/or line umpires have officiated a match for you, thank them for calling the match immediately after its conclusion. When you have concluded your performance in a tournament, you should find and thank the tournament director and members of the tournament committee for their efforts in conducting a well-organized event and for providing you with an enjoyable and educational experience.

SPECTATORS

Spectators should sit in the area provided for spectators, not on the courtside benches, the fences, or the court surface itself. Only if bleachers are not provided and if approval is obtained from tournament officials and all players involved in the match is it permissible for spectators to sit on the courtside benches. Those who choose to do so should be extremely careful to enter and leave the court enclosure when players are changing ends and preferably only at the beginning and end of the match.

Applaud good play after the point is completed, not in the middle of the rally because the player you are rooting for just made a great "get." Even though a spontaneous reaction may be unavoidable, wait until the point is over to applaud. Part of the tradition of tennis is to *applaud only the good shots made by either side* and never to boo the bad shots or the errors. This tradition stresses the positive approach. Applaud the good shots and keep quiet on the errors. This means you do not applaud if the team you favor wins a point on the other team's error.

If you are interested in the score, keep it yourself, and don't bother the players by continually asking the score. If there is no other way of determining the score, wait until the players change ends, then quietly ask one of them. Players, please note that if you would announce the score periodically, spectators would not have to bother you to find out! As a spectator, you are not supposed to coach or kibitz with the players. Their concentration is essential to their performance, and they will thank you to keep still.

Spectators should not act in the capacity of line umpires. The players are responsible for calling their own lines and should make their own decisions. Rarely is a spectator in good position to make an accurate call on close balls. Therefore, even if a player asks, say nothing or say that you can't call it. If there are line umpires on the match, it is extremely poor behavior for spectators to "second guess" the line umpire's call. The line umpire is in the best possible position to make the call; and you will do everyone a favor by accepting the decision and by not trying to influence the call or to upset the players. The line umpire has volunteered and frequently serves without remuneration of any kind. Avoid subjecting officials to any kind of abuse. If you wish to improve what you consider to be a poor situation, learn how to call lines—it's not hard—and volunteer your services; then the lines will be called to your satisfaction!

Both on and off the courts, you will find that courteous manners and sportsmanlike behavior contribute to everyone's enjoyment of the game as well as to the great tennis tradition itself.

8 The Language and Lore of Tennis

To provide a taste and some of the flavor of the game, there is included here a descriptive list of some of the more interesting words, the aim of which is to whet your appetite and to spur you on to further study. The list of selected references (p. 126) includes several books and periodicals which will be helpful to you. In general, this chapter contains those terms which have not been described elsewhere in the book. Where duplication does occur, the brief definitions presented here are supplemented by references (the numbers in parentheses) to the chapter(s) in which further information may be found.

Ace   An exceptionally good service, served so well that the receiver cannot reach it; an outright winner.

American twist   An advanced serve in which the racket strikes the ball with an upward and sideward motion causing the ball to spin during its flight and to take a high bounce, usually to the receiver's backhand (3).

Approach shot   The type of shot, usually a groundstroke, behind which a player advances to the net position, usually one hit deep into the opponent's court with medium speed (5).

ATP   Association of Tennis Professionals. An organization of male professional tennis players (9).

Backcourt   The area between the service line and the baseline (1).

Backspin   Spin applied to the ball by hitting down behind it, causing the ball to spin in the opposite direction from its flight (3).

Baseline game   A type of strategy employed by a player who remains near the baseline and attempts to outsteady the opponent (5).

Break point   The point which, if won by the receiver, breaks the opponent's serve; a very important point for both players. See *service break*.

Bye   A term commonly used in single elimination tournaments to indicate that a player does not have to play in the first round. The number of byes is determined by subtracting the number of entries from the next higher power of two. USTA tournament regulations prescribe the location of the byes in the draw.

Challenge round   The last round of a challenge-type tournament. The Davis Cup was the primary example of this type of tournament in which the champion nation of the preceding year waited while all of the challenging nations played a series of elimination tournaments. The winner of the elimination tournament became the challenger and played the champion in the *challenge round*. In 1972, the Davis Cup format changed to a single elimination tournament.

Chip   A term applied to short, angled shots, mostly sliced returns of serve in doubles (3).

Chop   A stroke in which the racket is drawn down and under the ball imparting backspin to it (3).

Consolation tournament   Held in connection with a single elimination tournament for first round (sometimes first and second round) losers (10).

Continental grip   Sometimes called the service grip. Players who use this grip usually do not change grips for the forehand and backhand drives, but use this one grip to hit all shots (2, 3).

Crosscourt   A shot in which the ball travels over the net from one corner to the corner diagonally opposite (5).

Davis Cup   A large silver trophy donated by Dwight Davis in 1900. Originally, the trophy was presented to the winner of a series of men's team matches between the United States and England. Now, between 50 and 60 nations compete for the Davis Cup each year. Each team match (called a tie) follows a prescribed format of two singles matches on the first day, a doubles match on the second day, and two more singles matches on the third day. A nation must win three of the five matches to defeat its opposing nation. Each individual match is the best of five sets. See *challenge round*. Davis Cup competition begins early in the year and often is not completed until December. In 1980, the ITF adopted a new format in which the top sixteen teams comprise the World Group and compete in a single elimination tournament. Other nations enter one of four zonal competitions with the zonal winners advancing into the World Group in the following year.

Dead ball   A ball which has lost air pressure and consequently does not rebound as well as a normal or live ball. Poor stroke habits may result from using dead balls (1, 9).

Deep   A term used to describe a shot that lands within the court near the baseline. A deep serve is one that lands within the service court near the service line (5).

Default   A player who fails to play a tournament match loses by default; the opponent moves into the next round.

Dink   To hit the ball with an extreme margin of error, usually quite high over the net, and quite deep into the opponent's court at a moderate or low rate of speed. This type of player is often called a retriever and relies on an ability to get the ball back often enough so that the opponent will eventually make an error (5).

Double elimination tournament   A type of tournament in which a player must lose two matches before being eliminated from the tournament (10).

Double fault   Loss of a point by the server for failing to make good on either of the two chances to serve (6).

Down-the-line   A shot in which the ball travels over the net close and parallel to a sideline (5).

Draw   The organization of competitors in a tournament; in the typical single elimination tournament, each entrant's name is placed on a separate card, and the cards are then drawn at random. The names are entered on the tournament chart in the order drawn (except for the seeded entrants). You may hear discussion about attending the draw—the meeting at which the committee actually draws the names from the hat. (Attend a draw sometime—it's very interesting.) You may also hear players asking one another "Have you seen the draw?" and in this case they are referring to the posted tournament chart listing the entrants in the order drawn. Players will also talk about the "luck of the draw" referring to the quality of the opposing players drawn into their quarter or half of the tournament. A player with a "tough" draw must meet a high-caliber opponent in an early round, while a player with a "good" draw meets opponents who are less well-known and against whom there is a good chance of winning.

Drive   Usually refers to a ball hit after the bounce with a full stroke so that it travels fairly fast from one end of the court to the other (2).

Drop shot   A ball hit softly with backspin so that it just clears the net and lands close to the net with a low bounce (3, 5).

Drop volley   Very similar to the dropshot but executed as a volley instead of a groundstroke (3, 5).

Earned point   A point won by skillful playing rather than through an opponent's error (5).

Eastern grip   The forehand and backhand grips as presented (2).

Error   A point lost through a mistake not caused by your opponent (5). There are basically two ways in which a point can be won: Either you play so well and hit such an unbeatable shot that your opponent couldn't be expected to make a return, or you play poorly or carelessly and miss a return that normally could be made. The experts say that many more points are lost on errors than are won on placements or on earned points.

Even court   The right court, since whenever play is started in this court, an even number of points has been played in the current game (6). Note that the two right service courts are diagonally opposite each other (1).

Face   The strings of the racket which are the hitting surface (1). A *closed face* refers to the angle of the racket face when the top edge is turned forward so that the hitting surface faces down toward the ground. An *open face* refers to the angle of the racket face when the top edge is turned backward so that the hitting surface faces up toward the sky (2). See also *flat*.

Fault   A technical term indicating an illegal return or serve; much more commonly used to indicate a serve that lands outside of the proper service court (6).

Federation Cup   International team competition for women which was started in 1963 by the ILTF (now the ITF). A single elimination team tournament is held over a period of four or five days. Two singles matches and one doubles match constitute a team match, and the nation that wins at least two of the three matches advances to the next round of the tournament.

Fifteen   Term used in scoring to indicate the first point won by a player in each game (6). The origin of this term is based on early scoring systems in which a player had to make 15 chases to win one point.

Finals   The last or final round of a single elimination tournament in which two players in a singles event or two teams in a doubles event compete for the championship.

Five   Commonly used abbreviation for fifteen.

Flat   *Flat face* is a term used to describe the position of the racket head when the face is perpendicular to the court and faces the net squarely, sometimes called *square face*. A *flat drive* is produced with a flat face and a level swing, thus directing the ball in a fairly straight trajectory with little arc and little or no spin. The term *flat* is also used to describe a serve hit with no spin (2, 3, 5).

Foot fault   A violation of the service rule, usually occurring when a player steps on or over the baseline, although illegal movement of the feet is also a foot fault (6).

Forcing shot   A strong attacking shot, usually fast, deep, and well placed, designed to force either an error or a weak return from your opponent (5).

Forecourt   The area between the net and the service line (1).

Grand Prix   A series of tournaments in which players earn points based on their performance; at the end of the season, the top 8 point winners compete in a single elimination masters championship (10).

Grand Slam   Winning in the same year what some experts consider to be the four major tennis events in the world, the Championships of Australia, France, England (Wimbledon), and the United States (formerly Forest Hills, now the U.S. Open held at the USTA National Tennis Center, Flushing Meadow). Don Budge, Maureen Connolly, Rod Laver (twice), and Margaret Court are the only players to have accomplished this feat. Martina Navratilova has won the four Grand Slam events in succession, but not in the same calendar year.

Groundstroke   A stroke, usually the forehand or backhand drive, used to hit a ball after it has bounced (2).

Half volley   A defensive stroke used to hit the ball immediately after it has bounced. Usually, a player is forced to hit a half volley due to being unable to reach a position in the forecourt from which a volley, a much stronger shot, can be made (3).

Head   The frame and strings of the racket (1). Also, that part of the anatomy which many players neglect to use! (5)

Hold service   When the server wins the game. If you hold your serve every time, you cannot lose a set (5, 6).

ITF   The International Tennis Federation (1, 6); the organization that governs tennis competition throughout the world.

Left court (player)   The partner of a doubles team who receives service in the left court. The left court is also referred to as the odd court, the ad court, or the backhand court, since usually the player with the stronger backhand plays the left court.

Let   A serve which hits the top of the net but is otherwise good. A let serve is re-served. Also, a point that is interrupted by interference, in which case the point is played over (6).

Lob   A ball hit so that its flight goes high into the air (usually over the reach of the net player) and deep in the opponent's backcourt. A *lob volley* has a similar trajectory but is hit before the ball has bounced and is considered to be a very advanced and very delicate shot (3, 5).

Loop   Refers to balls hit with topspin, because the flight of the ball seems to dip sharply; also used to refer to players who stroke their shots with a "loopy," as contrasted with a level swing (2).

Love   Term used in scoring to mean zero or nothing. This word probably came from the French word "l'oueff" which means goose egg, and when the game was taken to England, the French word was pronounced like "love." A *love game* is won without the loss of a point, and if you win a *love set* you have won six games, and your opponent has won none. When you are told that a player has won a match "love and love," this means the opponent did not win a game (6).

Match point   The point which, if won by the player who is ahead, wins the match. A tenacious player might fight off match points held by the opponent and hang on to win the match.

Mixed doubles   A type of competition in which a man and woman play as partners against another doubles team composed in the same manner.

Net game   A type of strategy employed by a player who attempts to reach a position in the forecourt in order to utilize volleys and overheads to win points (5).

Netman (net player)   Usually used in doubles to refer to the partner of the server who plays near the net (5).

"No-man's land"   The midcourt area behind the service line where many balls will bounce at the player's feet, thus forcing attempts at difficult half volleys. It's dangerous there! Skilled players try to move through this area as quickly as possible (3, 5).

Not up   Refers to a double bounce. This term is used by an umpire when a player fails to play the ball before the second bounce.

Odd court   The left court, since whenever play is started in this court, an odd number of points has been played in the current game (6).

On the rise   The term used to describe an aggressive style of play in which a player returns the ball before it reaches the height of its bounce. By playing the ball early or on the rise, you give your opponent less time to get set for your return. This type of play is usually not advocated for beginners (2, 5).

Opening   An offensive opportunity, created either by your own forcing play or by your opponent's errors, which, if utilized properly, should reward you with a point (5).

Overhead smash   The advanced shot that is the answer to the lob. The stroke resembles the serve and is a hard overhead swing. It is sometimes referred to as a smash or as an overhead (3, 5).

Overspin   See *topspin.*

Passing shot   To hit the ball past the reach of a net player either down the line or crosscourt. One of the choices available to a backcourt player when an opponent rushes the net (5).

Poach   An advanced technique used in doubles play. As the net player, you leave your usual position, cross in front of your partner to "steal" a ball that would normally have been played by your partner. Look for this when you're watching the experts play, and note how the backcourt team tries to outguess the net player by lobbing or hitting down the line (5).

Put-away   A shot, also called a kill or a winner, that is hit so well no return is expected. A novice may try to put away every ball, but a more experienced player knows that you have to maneuver your opponent out of position before most put-away attempts will be successful (5).

Quarter finals   In a single elimination tournament, the round in which eight players remain in singles or eight teams in doubles; also called the round of eight.

Rally   Describes play after the serve to the conclusion of the point. Also a series of shots in which both players are able to keep the ball in play (5).

Rankings   At the end of each season, national and sectional associations place tournament players in rank order based upon their tournament performances during the preceding year (9).

Retrieve   Making a long run to return an opponent's good shot. A retriever is a player whose style of play is primarily defensive; that is, a player who relies on the ability to run down and return any shot that the opponent may hit and does not attempt to hit put-aways or risk the possibility of error (5).

Return   A generalized term applying to a ball hit back to your opponent. Sometimes the term is used more specifically to refer to the return of service. Since you cannot win a match unless you can break your opponent's serve, the return of serve is an extremely important aspect of the game (5).

Right court (player)   The partner of a doubles team who receives service in the right court. The right court is also referred to as the even court, the deuce court, or the forehand court.

Rough   Rough and smooth refer to the trimming strings that were formerly found around the racket strings near the tip and near the throat and were wound in such a way that on one hitting surface they felt smooth and on the other hitting surface they felt rough. These terms may be used in tossing a racket at the beginning of a match (6).

Round   Each round of a single elimination tournament is numbered until play reaches the quarter final, semifinal, and final rounds. First round play refers to the first matches played; at the end of the first round, half of the players who played are eliminated, and the winners of the first round matches move into the second round where the process is repeated.

Round robin   A type of tournament in which each player or team plays every other player or team; the winner is the entry that wins the greatest number of matches (10).

Rush the net   A style of play in which a player hits an approach shot and runs toward the net to be in a better position to win a point (5).

Seeding   A process by which the best or ranked entrants in a single elimination tournament are placed in the draw so that they will not meet each other in the early rounds of a tournament. The tournament committee, in effect, predicts the winner and seeds that player number one. The committee judges who will be the second best player and seeds that person number two. Usually, for every four entries, one player is seeded. The seeded players are then placed in specified positions in the draw. If the committee's predictions come true, the number one and number two seeded players will meet in the finals, and they will have defeated the number three and number four seeded players in the semifinals. Seedings are based on rankings and upon recent tournament performance. When a seeded player is defeated by an unseeded player, an upset has occurred.

Semifinals   In a single elimination tournament, the round in which four players remain in singles or four teams in doubles; also called the round of four. The winners of the two semifinal matches advance to the finals.

Service   The served ball itself; also referred to as a serve. Since the receiver must be ready before the serve is delivered, this term is sometimes used by impatient servers to recall the wandering attention of the receiver. It should not be used routinely before each point since its use implies that the receiver is slow or inattentive (7).

Service break   As the server if you fail to win the game you serve, the receiver breaks your serve. In order to win a set, you must break serve (5).

Set point   The point which, if won by the player who is ahead, wins the set (6).

Short-angle shot   A type of shot directed crosscourt toward the junction of your opponent's service line and sideline. It is very useful in maneuvering your opponent out of position (5).

Sidespin   When the ball spins on its vertical axis, like a top (3).

Single elimination tournament   The most common type of competition in which a player is eliminated as soon as one match is lost.

Slice   When this term is applied to a groundstroke or a volley, the ball is hit with backspin, and when applied to a serve, the ball is hit with sidespin (3).

Smash   Same as *overhead smash*.

Smooth   See *rough*.

Spin   When force is applied to the ball off center, the ball will spin (3, 5). See also *backspin, chip, chop, drop shot, drop volley, loop, sidespin, slice, topspin, twist*.

Stop volley   Same as *drop volley*.

Sudden death   The 5 of 9 point tiebreaker (6).

Sweet spot   An area of the strings usually located slightly below the center of the racket face. When the ball contacts the sweet spot, vibrations transmitted to the hand are minimal (9).

Tennis   Presumably derived from the French verb *tenez,* the imperative of *tenir,* which means to hold, take, or receive. Thus, the name of the game is inherent in the rules which require that the server must hold the attention of the receiver before the serve may be legally delivered (6).

Throat   That part of the racket just below the head. While the word "neck" may seem just as logical to a novice, it is not appropriate, and its use marks one as unacquainted with proper terminology (1).

Tiebreaker   A 7 of 12 point scoring system which can go into effect at 6 games all. Tiebreaker procedures have come into being in an attempt to reduce the length of tennis matches (6).

Topspin   Spin applied to the ball by hitting up behind it, causing the ball to spin in the same direction as its flight (3).

Toss the racket (spin the racket)   At the beginning of a match, a racket is "tossed" so that it lands flat on the ground. Formerly the terms rough and smooth were used in calling the toss; the winner (and the loser) of the toss make certain choices (6).

Trajectory   Refers to ball flight which is caused by the method of stroke production (2, 3). Understanding various trajectories and their attributes plays an important role in strategy and in making the correct choice of shot (5).

Twist   Usually refers to a type of serve hit with topspin; sometimes called the American twist serve (3).

Two-step   Step-together-step. A movement commonly used to make small adjustments in position. When moving to the right, make the first step with the right foot, bring the left foot up to it, and then step again on the right foot. This frees the left foot to step forward into the shot. Do the reverse when moving to the left (2).

Umpire   Usually called the chair umpire, this is the official who is in direct charge of a match, supervises the conduct of the line umpires and the players, announces the score at the conclusion of each point, and performs other duties as described in the USTA *Umpire's Manual.*

Underspin   Same as *backspin.*

Unseeded   A player who is not seeded, thus not favored to win or even to survive the early rounds of play. See *seeding.*

USLTA   The United States Lawn Tennis Association, which deleted the word "lawn" from its title in 1975. See *USTA.*

USPTA   The United States Professional Tennis Association. An organization of teaching professionals (more than 2800 certified members) designed to promote ethical standards and sound educational methods in tennis teachers.

USTA   The United States Tennis Association (9); formerly the USLTA.

Volley   A ball hit before it bounces (2) and an essential part of an attacking game (5).

WCT   World Championship of Tennis. One of the early promoters of modern professional tennis, now a highly competitive prize money circuit for men under contract to WCT (10).

Western Grip   The method of gripping the racket in which the racket is placed face down on the ground and the player merely picks it up and places the V on the back plate. A player who uses this grip hits balls on both left and right sides with the same grip and the same face of the racket. The Western grip is said to have originated on the hard-surfaced courts in the west where the surface caused high rebounds which can be hit very effectively with this grip. However, it is most ineffective for low-bouncing balls, and since some of the major tournaments are played on grass courts which tend to produce low rebounds, players with Western grips very rarely appear among those on the championship circuit. Further, the mechanical disadvantages inherent in this grip make it an inappropriate choice (2).

Wightman Cup   In 1919, Mrs. Hazel Hotchkiss Wightman, one of the most remarkable women in United States tennis history, donated a cup for international women's team competition. She proposed that competition be along Davis Cup lines and that it be open to all nations, but since considerable expense was involved, actual competition did not begin until 1923 and then only between the United States and England. Five singles matches and two doubles matches constitute a team match. The event is held each year, the site alternating between the two countries. At least four players are required to play the matches on a two-day schedule. The number one and number two singles players exchange singles opponents on the second day of play.

WITA   Women's International Tennis Association. An organization of women professional tennis players designed to improve tournament schedules, conditions of play, prize money, player rankings, and player health and pension plans (9).

9 Facts for Enthusiasts

SELECTING AND CARING FOR EQUIPMENT

The manufacture and sale of tennis equipment is a large, competitive industry. Some statistical reports claim that tennis is a billion dollar business. Without doubt, the "tennis boom" is a reality, as the number of people playing and watching the game continues to rise. Almost every manufacturer of tennis equipment reports increased sales over the past several years. While the basic equipment requirements are still a racket and a few tennis balls, the quality and cost of this equipment varies considerably. In addition, the purchaser will be confronted with a wide variety of "essential" accessories and thus must understand the options available in order to acquire equipment which is desirable and in an appropriate price range. A discussion of clothing and shoes has been presented in Chapter 1; this section will provide further information on rackets, strings and balls.

Rackets

Prior to the 1970s almost all tennis rackets were made of wood and were the same size and shape. They were 27 inches long and 9 inches wide across the face, and therefore two rackets could be used to measure the height of the net at its center (36″) (see fig. 7.1). Some models had been on the market virtually unchanged for 10 to 20 years. And then came the revolution in tennis equipment, with modern materials, different shapes, oversize heads, laboratory test ratings, play test ratings and an incredible, constantly changing, variety of models, as well as prices, from which to choose. For today's player, selecting a racket is a complex process.

Wooden racket frames vary in price and quality. This range reflects differences in the quality of wood used, the number of laminations in the head of the racket, and the quality of the material used on the grip. While the frame of a high-priced wood racket may appear to be a single piece of wood, closer inspection will reveal as many as 13 separate strips of wood and fiber (called ply) laminated together into a single unit by a bonding process. Often, a little sticker on the racket head frame will indicate 8-ply, 11-ply or some other number of ply, but you can count the number of strips for yourself. In general, the greater the number of strips there are, the higher the price of the racket. In addition, the quality of the wood influences the cost. Ash, maple, and several types of synthetic fibers are materials commonly used. The outside strip is usually a hardwood to increase durability. A hardwood, such as maple or beech is also used to make the throat of the racket. The handle is covered with leather, imitation leather, rubber or plastic grips. The best rackets use a good grade of leather, which is usually perforated and sometimes has raised ridges built in to permit better absorption of perspiration from the hand.

Many varieties of metal rackets are now on the market, and many companies are continuing experimentation with designs, materials, and production methods. Current designs utilize aluminum, chrome-plated special alloy steel, magnesium or titanium in the frame which usually has an open Y-shape throat. A leather grip covers the handle and conventional strings are used, although variations in string patterns and in string tension may be necessary. Graphite is one of the newer materials used in racket frame construction. The manufacturers claim that it is designed to combine the best qualities of both wood and metal. Rackets which are constructed mainly from graphite tend to be much more expensive than the average wood or metal racket, due to the cost of the materials and the construction process.

Several companies are producing rackets called composites, which can be made of any number of combinations such as wood and graphite, fiberglass and wood, graphite and fiberglass, etc. The prices of these rackets will vary considerably according to the type and amount of material used in their construction. Proponents of the new rackets claim many advantages, such as reduced air resistance, more power with less effort, more "feel," and reduced elbow strain. Other newer materials include Kevlar, boron, and ceramic fibers which are used primarily for reinforcement in racket frame construction.

Probably the most notable innovation has been the oversize racket head which in turn has produced a mid-size head. These rackets tend to offer less power and more control. According to the manufacturers, the bigger head provides for a larger hitting area thereby creating a "sweet spot" larger than the "sweet spot" in regular-size rackets. Manufacturers also claim that the larger racket heads tend to produce less vibration and absorb more shock.

In addition to the above material and price considerations, rackets come with varying weights, grip sizes, and balance points. Most rackets weigh between 12 and 15 ounces and are classified as light, medium, or heavy. Lightweight rackets (12 to 13 ounces) are appropriate for children, most women and some men. Medium-weight rackets (13½ to 13¾ ounces) are used by some women and most men, and heavyweight rackets (14 to 15 ounces) are usually used by very strong men. Other things being equal, the heavier the racket is, the greater the force imparted to the ball. The more weighty racket is, therefore, a more efficient tool than the lighter racket, but *only* if the player is strong enough to use it correctly. The player who attempts to use a racket which is too heavy is very susceptible to faulty stroke habits, unnecessary fatigue, and general discouragement.

The grip size is determined by measuring the circumference of the grip. People with small hands should choose a smaller grip size (4¼", 4⅜" or 4½"), a medium-sized hand needs about a 4⅝" grip, and a large hand requires a 4¾" or 5" grip. To determine the correct size for your hand, hold the racket firmly with the forehand grip (V on top plate, fingers spread comfortably). The tip of the second finger should be about even with the knuckle of the thumb. If the end of the second finger is even with your thumbnail, the grip is too large, and if the second finger presses into the base of your thumb, the grip is too small.

Although leather grips are still by far the most popular, many variations of grip materials are available, such as rubber, a spongelike material, terry cloth, felt or suede, and a gauze material which is used by wrapping it over an existing grip. Usually these variations are used by people with an extreme problem of perspiration on their hand, which in turn causes the racket to slip or turn while hitting the ball. Players who produce their strokes with two hands on the racket usually have the length of the leather grip extended.

The balance point of the racket is in the center of its length, 13½ inches from either end. Most rackets are evenly balanced, but baseline players usually prefer a head-heavy racket, while volleyers usually prefer a racket light in the head. Place the balance point of your racket on your index finger to see what kind of balance it has.

Racket flexibility is also an important consideration, because flexibility is one factor which differentiates all rackets, no matter what their composition or construction. Generally, the more flexible the racket, the more shock will be absorbed by the frame. Also, the flex in rackets will help dampen vibration created by off-center hits (fairly common among beginners!). Usually more flexible rackets are appropriate for slow courts and people who need added power; stiffer rackets are better for fast courts and big hitters.

The player should use a racket *only* for the purpose for which it was intended—to hit a tennis ball. The manufacturer did not intend for it to be thrown in any manner, nor was it made to be hit against the fence, the net post, the umpire's stand, or a hard-surfaced court. When not in use, the racket needs to be protected, primarily from moisture and from warping. It should be kept in a waterproof cover, which also keeps out the dust and allows the racket to be hung from the tab on the end of the cover. It may also be stored on a flat surface (lying on the shelf or on the floor of a closet—someplace where it cannot be stepped on easily), or it may be supported by pegs at its throat. The best way to promote warping is to store the racket standing on its head in the corner of your damp locker or even in the corner of a hot, dry closet. Do not store your racket in the trunk of your car for any length of time. The extreme temperatures (hot and cold) that can occur not only tend to age the frame unnecessarily but also can cause strings to break much sooner than they should. If you treat your racket well, you will gain many hours of pleasurable tennis from its use.

Strings

Rackets usually have 18 long strings and 21 cross strings. One company has recently increased the number of long strings to 20 and advertises that the denser stringing gives increased "feel" and control. Another company reduced the number of strings and advertises that fewer strings allow for more control. Generally, most stringing patterns have 18 long strings and 21 cross strings with only a 1- or 2-string variation. All rackets are strung with gut, nylon, or the newer synthetic gut. Most players prefer gut because it possesses greater resiliency and thus more snap when the ball is contacted. Gut is available in several degrees of thickness. Some tournament players use 17-gauge gut, the thinnest, least durable, but most resilient; most tournament players use 16-gauge, although 15-gauge is appropriate for the majority of weekend, public park, and club players.

Usually, when a player desires gut stringing, it is strung to order at a specific tension which may vary between 50 and 70 pounds. The type of racket and the size of the racket head should also be considered when selecting string tension. The average player would probably do well to determine appropriate string tension in consultation with the racket stringer and following the racket manufacturer's recommended guidelines.

Gut is very susceptible to moisture, and sometimes even brief exposure to dampness will cause the strings to swell and snap. Most tournament players carry two, three, or more matched rackets just in case the racket strings break during a match. Since play must be continuous, there can be no intermission while a racket string is being repaired, and playing with a broken string is detrimental both to the racket and to the player's performance! Gut is considerably more expensive than nylon. Nylon is moisture-proof, relatively durable, and quite elastic. It can be strung to a prescribed, but lesser, tension than gut, but will soon stretch slightly, thus losing its initial tension and some of its original snap when the ball is contacted.

One of the newest and more popular innovations is known as synthetic gut. Although it is a nylon, synthetic gut is so named because its playing characteristics are similar to gut yet its durability is closer to a basic nylon. It tends to be more resilient; some are textured, so that they seem to "grab" the ball better than other nylons. In cost, synthetic gut is in between the high-priced gut and the lower-priced nylon. Most school rackets are strung with nylon since it is satisfactory for beginners and provides good performance at a reasonable cost.

Choose a racket with the head size, weight, flex, and grip size appropriate for your size and strength, string tension appropriate to your skill level, balance point appropriate to your type of game, and quality appropriate to your budget. Many fine hours of tennis can be yours with a carefully selected, *appropriate,* and relatively inexpensive racket.

Balls

As you may recall from the brief discussion of tennis balls in Chapter 1, some tennis balls are molded around compressed air for resilience. These are known as pressurized balls, and almost all brands are sold three to an airtight plastic container. Pressurized tennis balls come in a number of different types. Heavy duty balls are designed for abrasive hard court use which is normally found outdoors. Normal or regular felt balls have a less durable cover and are designed for play on less abrasive hard courts (usually indoors) and clay. High altitude balls are specifically produced for high altitude play. The bounce is reduced because the thin atmosphere makes a normal ball too lively for comfortable play. Pressurized balls will last from 3 to 9 sets, depending on a number of factors: how hard the ball is hit, how much spin is used, what type of surface is played on, the temperature and humidity. Cold temperatures tend to "deaden" balls, but they will liven up by either playing with them or moving them to a warmer storage area. In order to maintain air pressure within the balls, pressurized containers should not be opened until the balls will be used in order to prevent loss of pressure or "dead" balls.

Balls made without the compressed air center achieve their resilience from rubber centers and are commonly known as pressureless balls. Pressureless balls are noticeably heavier and do not bounce quite as high. They are less susceptible to the effects of heat and cold and last considerably longer than pressurized balls. Pressureless balls are usually packaged 3 or 4 to a cardboard box container and retain their bounce indefinitely. The heavy-duty ball or the nonpressurized ball is probably the best buy for a beginner, since most experts recommend learning the game with heavy balls, that is, balls which have retained their original weight and have not become light as a result of wearing down the felt cover until only the skin is left. Tennis balls are numbered for easier identification in case one of your balls strays onto a neighboring court where others are using the same brand.

Several different types of ball preservers or ball pressurizers are available. They prevent a used ball from losing any more pressure after the can has been opened, but none is capable of restoring new life into a dead ball. For the occasional player, ball preservers can aid in extending the life of an already opened, but not worn out, can of balls.

Weight, balance, and flexibility are among the factors to be considered in selecting a racket. Why might a player find the following characteristics desirable: light weight? head-heavy balance? more flexibility?

TENNIS ORGANIZATIONS

The official governing body of tennis in this country is the United States Tennis Association. The USTA is made up of member tennis clubs from throughout the nation; the nation is subdivided into 17 sections, each of which has its own sectional association. (Consult Appendix 3 for USTA and sectional association addresses.) USTA voting rights are granted only to direct member clubs and to the sectional associations.

A new category of individual membership was adopted by the USTA in 1978; this includes adult membership (21 years of age and older), junior (under 21), family, life, and honorary memberships. Payment of dues allows individual members to compete in USTA-sanctioned tournaments, makes individuals eligible for national and sectional rankings, and provides subscriptions to a newspaper published approximately every four weeks called *Tennis, USA* and to *World Tennis,* a monthly magazine.

Some of the functions of the USTA are listed below.

1. It publishes and distributes the official rules in the *USTA Official Yearbook,* an annual publication, and it maintains a rules interpretation service. USTA rules are used universally throughout this country.
2. It conducts, supervises, and *sanctions* both amateur and professional (prize money) tournaments. Certain standards must be met and tournament regulations followed by the committee of a sanctioned tournament.
3. It establishes the national rankings of United States players on the basis of their participation in sanctioned tournaments, including the major grass court tournaments played at private clubs in the Eastern section, sometimes referred to as the "grass court circuit," and the open prize money events. In

1986, the USTA established national rankings in 62 categories, including boys, girls, men and women in singles and doubles, from ages 12 and under to ages 80 and over.

4. It represents this nation in the ITF, the International Tennis Federation. This organization is responsible for conducting Davis Cup and Federation Cup matches, and other international events.

5. For this nation it presides over the Davis Cup, Federation Cup, Wightman Cup, and other international team programs. Selecting, training, and financing the U.S. teams which compete in these international events are the responsibilities of the USTA.

6. As the national governing body of tennis, the USTA represents tennis on the United States Olympic Committee and the Pan American Games Committee. Currently, tennis is played as part of the Pan American Games, the World University Games and in 1988, tennis will once again become an official sport of the Olympic Games.

7. Primarily through the Center for Education and Recreational Tennis (see Appendix 3 for address), the USTA provides many services to the tennis playing community in general, for example, free and inexpensive materials, film rentals, junior development programs, Junior Wightman Cup and Junior Davis Cup programs for promising younger players, as well as clinics and workshops for tennis instructors.

8. The USTA establishes rules which determine amateur and professional player status. An amateur is one who has received no monetary gain by playing, teaching, or demonstrating the game, although there are certain exceptions. Some of these are given below.

   a. A touring tennis player is permitted to receive a certain amount of money to defray expenses. The ITF specifies the maximum which may be paid to a player.

   b. A student in regular attendance at college may be employed during vacation periods as a camp counselor, a tennis professional's assistant, or a club employee; *however,* pay must be on a weekly or monthly *salary* basis, not on an hourly or per lesson basis.

   c. Regular members of a school or college faculty are allowed to teach tennis as a part of their faculty assignment, or coach, if they are also regular members of the faculty.

   d. A high school or college student may be the recipient of a scholarship or other benefits provided by the school or college being attended.

NOTE: The current *USTA Yearbook* should be consulted for the rules governing amateur status in effect at any given time.

9. It conducts a schools program which aims to introduce tennis to every school child in the nation.

Each sectional association is the voice of the USTA for its specific area. The sectional association assists in the formation of clubs, sanctions tournaments for the area, supervises the scheduling of tournament dates, determines the sectional rankings of its players, assists its champions to compete in national tournaments, operates junior development programs, administers USTA membership for the area, and provides other similar services. Members of the sectional associations are also members of the USTA and are the private clubs, colleges and institutions of the area.

Another type of tennis organization is administered by municipal and county recreation departments. The NPPTA (National Public Parks Tennis Association), sponsors a national tournament which moves to a different location each year. This tournament has a USTA sanction but limits participation to public park players, that is, those who do not belong to private clubs.

The United States Professional Tennis Association (USPTA) is an organization of professional tennis teachers. Certified members have demonstrated knowledge of tennis, skill in playing the game, and mastery of sound teaching methods appropriate for both private and group instruction. In addition to other activities, the USPTA promotes ethical standards among its members and has endorsed a Tennis Academy which provides basic courses for aspiring tennis teachers and advanced courses for members who wish to improve their teaching and business skills. The USPTA also maintains a job placement bureau to increase the career opportunities of its members and to assist potential employers in finding professionally qualified and responsible personnel for position openings.

The Association of Tennis Professionals (ATP) for men and the Women's International Tennis Association (WITA) are organizations of professional tennis players who compete in the prize money tournaments. Members of each of these organizations come from many countries throughout the world. These organizations serve as a unifying force for the players, represent players in their negotiations with tournament promoters, and provide current computerized rankings of the players based on tournament results.

As you look ahead to a lifetime of participation in tennis, two relatively new organizations will welcome your membership, the Senior Women's Tennis Association and Super Senior Tennis for men over 55. Each of these organizations promotes camaraderie, competition, products, and political positions favorable to senior players.

SPECTATOR TENNIS

Increasing interest in tennis has convinced promoters and advertisers that tennis can help to sell their products. Consequently, more companies are sponsoring tennis events both live and on television. Countless hours of tennis are telecast nationally by major commercial networks and the Public Broadcasting Service. This kind of exposure, with increased opportunity to watch the top players play excellent tennis, has served to increase the public interest. Today's beginner can watch the experts play exciting points and matches, listen to commentators discussing the fine points of rule and strategy, and receive topflight instruction on strokes without even leaving the room.

In addition to television tennis, there are increasing numbers of prize money tournaments for the topflight players. In 1985, the Grand Prix circuit for men staged 69 tournaments in 23 countries around the world while the Virginia Slims Women's Tour held 52 events. Many of these competitions were held in the United

States. The professional Grand Champions Tour for men over 35, the Grand Masters for men over 45, and futures tours for topflight amateurs and aspiring pros all provide opportunities for you to become a tennis spectator. Watch for them to appear near your community and have a look at excellent tennis up close and in person!

As a spectator, study the methods of stroke production, styles and strategy of play, the interaction of opponent personalities; take your eyes off the ball and study one player for several minutes to observe preparation, follow-through and recovery. Try watching tennis matches from various vantage points—at court level, looking down from balcony levels, from the sides and from the ends of the court. You will probably be able to analyze strategy more effectively from the ends. Visualize yourself as "the coach" of one of the players and analyze strengths and weaknesses of the performance. What advice would you give? How would you play the match? You may discover an aptitude for a new career or you may become an increasingly keen and knowledgeable fan!

There are also many exciting amateur tournaments, including park, club, and sectional events for all ages and skill levels, played in local communities throughout the nation. It may be of special interest for you to observe the junior tournaments, and over the years, to watch some of the younger players develop. As you watch the twelve-year-olds play, can you predict who will be winning the 18's? or the opens? or the seniors?!

Review the section of Chapter 7 which presents spectator etiquette so that whenever you are a spectator, your behavior will contribute to a positive enjoyable experience for both the players and for other spectators.

Assume you are discussing how to be a good spectator *with other tennis players. Make a list of the points you would cover.*

10   Playing the Game

WHERE CAN YOU PLAY?

There are many different types of facilities for playing tennis, each with its own set of customs and regulations which you will want to follow. Most high schools and colleges have their own courts, and while these are reserved for classes during certain hours, they are usually available to students for extra practice and recreational play when classes are not in session. Since classes have priority, be sure to leave quickly and graciously when an instructor asks you to do so. If there should be an extra court available, most instructors will be happy to have you continue your game, providing, of course, you do not distract the class.

Almost all communities provide public tennis courts in parks and other recreational areas. These are usually operated by municipal or county recreation departments. Typically, these courts are open to the public, although residents of the particular community may have priority. Some public courts are simply there, and it's first come, first served. Other public courts are operated on a reservation basis, and you have to phone or visit the office to secure a reservation which may entitle you to play for one or two specified hours. When courts are lighted for night play, the policies regarding their use may differ from those in effect during the day. If you are new in a community, call the local recreation department office to find out what the local policies are. This office can also tell you what kinds of organized tennis programs are being operated and can usually introduce you to the tennis-playing members of the community.

Sometimes an individual family will have a private tennis court in their backyard. You don't play there unless you are invited. The same thing holds for most private tennis clubs. You don't play there unless you are a member or unless a member invites you to be a guest. If you would like to join a private club, it is perfectly proper to inquire at the club office about the availability, cost, and eligibility requirements for membership. Most private clubs have several types of memberships, including family, individual, and junior, each with its own set of privileges and charges. Clubs that have multiple facilities, such as, golf, tennis, swimming, and the like, frequently offer memberships for golf alone or tennis alone, and, again, each type of membership will have specified costs and privileges. If you join a private club, abide by the privileges and responsibilities of membership that have been established. The tremendous growth of indoor court facilities, especially in wintry climates, has been paralleled by a great increase in the number of tennis participants, which a recent U.S. survey has shown to be more than 13 million.

Many of these 13 million individuals seek playing opportunities away from their local communities. Thus, the tennis resort, the great vacation getaway, provides tennis enthusiasts opportunities for play in numerous exotic settings. Tennis travel directories are recent additions to the publications offered by pro shops and book stores, and tennis holidays are frequently packaged into weekend and/ or week-long programs to include meals, lodging, tennis instruction, and court time. Many major hotels advertise the excellence and number of tennis courts available to their guests, and the businessperson carrying tennis rackets and briefcase is no stranger to modern airline travelers. Summer camps, weekend workshops, tennis tours to Europe and other parts of the world are also available. Study the options in both costs and services, plan carefully, and have an enjoyable tennis vacation!

WHAT KIND OF COMPETITION IS AVAILABLE?

All kinds of competition are available, no matter what your age, sex, or skill level. The USTA and many sectional associations sanction tournaments in the following age divisions: 12 and under, 14 and under, 16 and under, 18 and under, 21 and under; open; for men, 35 and over, 40 and over, 45, 50, 55, 60 65, 70, 75 and 80; and for women, 35 and over, 40 and over, 45, 50, 55, 60, 65 and 70! Whatever your age, there is a place for you!

There are five standard events in most adult tournaments: Men's Singles, Women's Singles, Men's Doubles, Women's Doubles, and Mixed Doubles. In addition, some enterprising tournament committees run events such as husband-and-wife mixed doubles, father-and-son doubles, mother-and-daughter doubles, father-and-daughter doubles, mother-and-son doubles, and veteran mixed doubles (the combined ages of both players must be 70 or over).

In some parts of the country, "classified" tournaments are held for players of varying skill levels. It works this way: Players are classified A, B, C, and D, with A as the highest classification and D the lowest or novice classification. An A player may enter A events only, but a B player may enter either or both A and B events. Thus, players of a given classification are permitted to play at their own level or at a higher level, but not at a lower level. This gives the beginners, those with little or no tournament experience, a chance to compete with others of comparable ability. In some places, you may enter a D or novice event only once; the next time you enter, you must play a higher classification. Sometimes, you retain your classification until you reach the finals of a tournament at that level, and then you are automatically reclassified at the next higher level. Classification policies vary considerably, but the object is to provide lots of action for people of similar skills and experience.

The recently developed *National Tennis Rating Program* may be of assistance to you, both in your local play and as you travel about the country. Originally designed to be a simple self-rating procedure, this program provides a classification system that will enable you to describe your skill level so that you and others can determine appropriate and compatible entry levels for social tennis events, lessons, league play, or other programs (fig. 10.1). Currently, the USTA is developing a staff of regional raters who will verify player ratings and attempt to improve the consistency of the ratings. In many parts of the country, tournaments and leagues are structured for "rated" players (i.e., a 4.0 league or a 4.5 tournament), and in the future, this program may replace the classification system (A, B, C, and D) described earlier.

If you are a student, you can get a good start in tournament play by entering your school or college intramural tournament. Drop by the intramural or physical education department office and find out when it will be held, how to enter, and how it operates. Usually, intramural tournaments are of the single elimination type. Once you lose, you're out; but occasionally, especially if the entry is large enough, consolation or double elimination tournaments are organized. In double elimination tournaments, you have to lose twice before you are out, an arrangement which gives you a chance to recover in case a "bad day" contributed to your first loss. In a consolation event, all the first round (sometimes first and second round) losers are placed in a separate event. This and the classification system described above serve similar purposes.

Many school and colleges also sponsor tennis teams for men and for women. Interscholastic and intercollegiate team competition can provide a tremendous backlog of match-play experience and many very enjoyable friendships. A typical intercollegiate team match consists of six singles matches and three doubles matches. The best players of each team play in the number one singles match, the second-best players play the number two singles match, and so on. Each match

---

National Tennis Rating Program

SELF-RATING GUIDELINES

The National Tennis Rating Program provides a simple, initial self-placement method of grouping individuals of similar ability levels for league play, tournaments, group lessons, social competition and club or community programs.

The rating categories are generalizations about skill levels. You may find that you actually play above or below the category which best describes your skill level, depending on your competitive ability. The category you choose is not meant to be permanent, but may be adjusted as your skills change or as your match play demonstrates the need for reclassification.

To Place Yourself:

A. Begin with 1.0. Read all categories carefully and then decide which one best describes your present ability level.

B. Be certain that you qualify on all points of all preceding categories as well as those in the classification you choose.

C. When rating yourself assume you are playing against a player of the same sex and the same ability.

D. Your self-rating may be verified by a teaching professional, coach, league coordinator or other qualified expert.

E. The person in charge of your tennis program has the right to reclassify you if your self-placement is thought to be inappropriate.

FIGURE 10.1 The National Tennis Rating Program (Reprinted by permission of the USTA)

THE NATIONAL
TENNIS RATING PROGRAM

1.0   This player is just starting to play tennis.

1.5   This player has limited playing experience and is still working primarily on getting the ball over the net; has some knowledge of scoring but is not familiar with basic positions and procedures for singles and doubles play.

2.0   This player may have had some lessons but needs on-court experience; has obvious stroke weaknesses but is beginning to feel comfortable with singles and doubles play.

2.5   This player has more dependable strokes and is learning to judge where the ball is going; has weak court coverage or is often caught out of position, but is starting to keep the ball in play with other players of the same ability.

3.0   This player can place shots with moderate success; can sustain a rally of slow pace but is not comfortable with all strokes; lacks control when trying for power.

3.5   This player has achieved stroke dependability and direction on shots within reach, including forehand and backhand volleys, but still lacks depth and variety; seldom double faults and occasionally forces errors on the serve.

4.0   This player has dependable strokes on both forehand and backhand sides; has the ability to use a variety of shots including lobs, overheads, approach shots and volleys; can place the first serve and force some errors; is seldom out of position in a doubles game.

4.5   This player has begun to master the use of power and spins; has sound footwork; can control depth of shots and is able to move opponent up and back; can hit first serves with power and accuracy and place the second serve; is able to rush net with some success on serve in singles as well as doubles.

5.0   This player has good shot anticipation; frequently has an outstanding shot or exceptional consistency around which a game may be structured; can regularly hit winners or force errors off of short balls; can successfully execute lobs, drop shots, half volleys and overhead smashes; has good depth and spin on most second serves.

5.5   This player can execute all strokes offensively and defensively; can hit dependable shots under pressure; is able to analyze opponents' styles and can employ patterns of play to assure the greatest possibility of winning points; can hit winners or force errors with both first and second serves. Return of serve can be an offensive weapon.

6.0   This player has mastered all the above skills; has developed power and/or consistency as a major weapon; and can vary strategies and styles of play in a competitive situation. This player typically has had intensive training for national competition at junior or collegiate levels.

6.5   This player has mastered all of the above skills and is an experienced tournament competitor who regularly travels for competition and whose income may be partially derived from prize winnings.

7.0   This is a world class player.

is the best two out of three sets, and the winner of each match scores one point for the team. Each coach arranges team personnel into the three strongest possible doubles combinations and ranks them in order of ability to play against the opposing school's doubles teams. The team winning the greatest number of points wins the match. Usually, colleges within a league or conference play a round robin type of schedule, that is, each college plays every other college to determine the conference standings. In some leagues, players may play singles and doubles, while in others, players may participate in only one event. Sometimes, a team match consists of five singles matches and two doubles matches or four singles matches and three doubles matches. The format varies, but it all adds up to many hours of enjoyable tennis.

Many other opportunities for competitive play exist within your locality. Most communities sponsor a city tennis championship, sometimes two. Only residents can enter the City Closed, but anyone can enter the City Open, unless it is restricted to amateurs only. If you belong to a tennis club, it will probably schedule several different types of tournaments throughout the year. A popular type of club tournament is the challenge ladder in which each entrant is assigned or drawn to a rung of the ladder. A player may challenge another player one, two, or three rungs above. The match is arranged at the convenience of both players, and, if the challenger wins, they trade places on the ladder, otherwise, both players stay in their original positions. There are many variations of the basic ladder tournament, so check the rules, which usually can be found posted next to the ladder itself.

Tournaments outside your local area frequently provide concomitant benefits inherent in traveling, meeting new people, visiting nearby scenic attractions, and, generally, enlarging and enriching your own private tennis world. Even the average player can gain from tennis travels to nearby communities and to the state and sectional championships in the area. These tournaments, however, are not appropriate for beginners, who should gain the necessary experience on the school, park, and local level. As you go up the tennis ladder, both national and international tournaments may bid for your participation as a competitor. Wimbledon, the U.S. Open, the French Championships, the Australian Championships, and major tournaments in many other nations throughout the world beckon those at the highest levels of skill.

Most of the world's high-ranking tennis players will agree that the greatest thrill in tennis is the opportunity to represent your nation in international team competition. The men and women who compete for the Davis Cup, the Wightman Cup, and the Federation Cup will long remember the inner excitement and pride when the umpire announces "game for the United States"!

Additional opportunities for playing the game are available to highly-skilled players who turn professional and subsequently compete for prize money. The development of professional tennis competition has been a fairly recent one, and the touring pros are much more highly organized now than they were formerly. In the past, two, three, or four players toured the country in a long series of exhibition matches, the winner being the player who won the greatest number of matches on the tour. In the early 1970s, World Championship of Tennis (WCT) promoted international tennis competition as a profit-making business venture.

Thirty-two of the world's leading male players were under contract to WCT, which guaranteed the players a minimum amount of money plus paying air fares to and from the various tournament sites. The contract pros competed for 35 to 45 weeks of the year for prize money which was earned in increasing amounts for each round won. Presumably, the best player was the one who won the most money. In 1971, Rod Laver won more than $200,000.

Increasing pressure for "open" tournaments in which top-ranking amateurs could compete against top-ranking professionals finally resulted in the world's first Open, in England, in April 1968 when one of the amateurs provided considerable excitement as he upset two highly-ranked professionals. The women, too, initiated their own pro tour under the sponsorship of *World Tennis Magazine* and Virginia Slims. Although the money available for prizes was not so great as that for men, the leading female money winner of 1971, Billie Jean King, exceeded her announced goal of earning $100,000 prize money in one year, the first woman in any sport to achieve that goal.

In the years since open tennis arrived, the tennis world has seen contract pros, independent pros, Women's Liberation, increasing prize money, the banning of players, the boycotting of tournaments, continuing problems, and some fantastic tennis. Prior to 1968, there were very few playing pros and prize money was minimal, but by 1974, prize money on the various circuits, the WCT, the Grand Prix, and the Virginia Slims Tour, was close to $8 million, and many players were seeking their share of the gold. More people were playing and watching better tennis than ever before.

As tennis moves to the end of the 1980s, we look back at a decade of phenomenal development and forward to a future of continuing change. Increasing opportunities for prize money competition are attracting ever greater numbers of players. In 1985, 240 men were included in the ATP computer rankings and 240 women were listed in the WITA computer rankings; these rankings determine which players are selected for entry into limited draw tournaments and are also utilized in seeding these tournaments. Tournament results are fed back into the computer and the rankings are revised immediately so that current rankings are readily available. The professional players associations have been instrumental in promoting satellite and futures championship circuits (usually with unlimited draws and open to all comers), so that younger, developing players (could you be one of them?!) have an opportunity to gain the necessary competitive experience and to qualify by playing for the major prize money championships.

The opportunities are there. The apparently unending increase in prize money, in addition to huge bonus pools distributed on the basis of performance during an entire season, plus enlarged tournament schedules have produced many $100,000-per-year players—more than 20 women and 35 men in 1985. Professional players have tournaments available to them every week of the year and frequently more than one. The season high earnings achieved by Laver and King in 1971 have been dwarfed by Ivan Lendl and Martina Navratilova who have each won more than $2,000,000 in a single season! Career earnings for John McEnroe exceed $8,000,000 and for Navratilova, $9,000,000. Several players, both men and women, have career earnings of more than two million dollars in tournament winnings and circuit bonuses.

IN CONCLUSION

This, then, has been a brief introduction to the wonderful world of tennis! Hopefully, the basic information provided here has inspired you with enough enthusiasm and excitement to make you a lifetime tennis participant and a permanent member of the tennis-minded community. Beyond the scope of this publication lies a much wider horizon. You can continue to expand your appreciation of the game by watching the experts, both amateurs and professionals, by reading books and periodicals suggested in the list of selected references, by taking group or private lessons from experienced teachers or professionals, by practicing and playing on your own with all kinds of opponents, and by joining and contributing to a local or national tennis organization. You, too, can belong, serve, and enjoy the worldwide game that is tennis today.

Selected References

BOOKS

Ashe, Arthur. *Arthur Ashe's Tennis Clinic.* Norwalk, Conn.: Golf Digest/Tennis, Inc. 1981.

Ashe, Arthur with Frank Deford. *Arthur Ashe: Portrait in Motion.* Boston: Houghton Mifflin Co., 1975.

Braden, Vic and Bill Bruns. *Vic Braden's Tennis for the Future.* Boston: Little, Brown and Co., 1977.

Brown, Jim. *Tennis: Strokes, Strategy, and Programs.* Englewood Cliffs, N.J.: Prentice-Hall, Inc., 1980.

Bryant, James E. *Game, Set, Match . . . A Beginning Tennis Guide.* Englewood, Colo.: Morton Publishing Co., 1986.

Cummings, Parke. *American Tennis.* Boston: Little, Brown and Co., 1957.

Gallwey, W. Timothy. *The Inner Game of Tennis.* New York: Random House, 1974.

Gensemer, Robert. *Intermediate Tennis.* Englewood, Colo.: Morton Publishing Co., 1985.

Gould, Dick. *Tennis, Anyone?* 4th ed. Palo Alto, Calif.: Mayfield Publishing Co., 1985.

Harman, Bob and Keith Monroe. *Use Your Head in Tennis.* Rev. ed. New York: Crowell, 1975.

King, Billie Jean and Greg Hoffman. *Tennis Love: A Parent's Guide to the Sport.* New York: Macmillan Publishing Co., Inc., 1978.

King, Billie Jean and Kim Chapin. *Tennis to Win.* New York: Harper and Row, 1970.

MacCurdy, Doug and Shawn Tully. *Sports Illustrated Tennis.* New York: Lippincott & Crowell, Time Inc., 1980.

McPhee, John. *Wimbledon: A Celebration.* New York: The Viking Press, 1972.

Mason, R. Elaine. *Tennis.* Boston: Allyn and Bacon, Inc., 1974.

Murphy, Bill. *Complete Book of Championship Tennis Drills.* West Nyack, N.Y.: Parker Publishing Co., Inc., 1975.

Murphy, Bill and Chet Murphy. *Tennis for Beginners.* New York: The Ronald Press Co., 1958.

Murphy, Chet. *Advanced Tennis.* 3rd ed. Dubuque, Ia.: Wm. C. Brown Publishers, 1982.

———. *Tennis for Thinking Players.* El Cerrito, Ca. Leisure Press, 1982.

Murphy, Chet and Bill Murphy. *Tennis for the Player, Teacher and Coach.* Philadelphia: W. B. Saunders Co., 1975.

Navratilova, Martina with Mary Carillo. *Tennis My Way.* New York: Charles Scribner's Sons, 1983.

Newcombe, John and Angie, with Clarence Mabry. *The Family Tennis Book.* Published by *Tennis Magazine* with Quadrangle. The New York Times Book Co., 1975.

Powel, N. E. *The Code.* Published by the United States Tennis Association. 1212 Avenue of the Americas, New York, N.Y. 10036. Reprinted 1985.

Ramo, Simon. *Extraordinary Tennis for the Ordinary Player.* New York: Crown Publishers, Inc., 1970.

Schulz, Charles M. *Snoopy's Tennis Book.* New York: Holt, Rinehart and Winston, 1979.

Shannon, Bill, ed. *United States Tennis Association Official Encyclopedia of Tennis.* New York: Harper and Row, 1981.

Smith, Stan and Bob Lutz with Larry Sheehan. *Modern Tennis Doubles.* New York: Atheneum/SMI, 1975.

Talbert, Bill with Gordon Greer. *Weekend Tennis*. Garden City, N.Y.: Doubleday and Co., Inc., 1970.

Talbert, William F. and Bruce S. Old. *Tennis Tactics Singles and Doubles*. New York: Harper and Row, 1983.

Tennis Magazine Editors. *Instant Tennis Lessons*. New York: Simon and Schuster, 1978.

————. *Tennis Strokes and Strategies*. New York: Simon and Schuster, 1975.

Tilden, William T., 2nd ed. *Match Play and the Spin of the Ball*. New York: American Lawn Tennis, 1925. Reprinted 1975.

United States Tennis Association. *USTA Official Yearbook*. 1212 Avenue of the Americas, New York, N.Y. 10036.

PERIODICALS

Tennis Industry Magazine. Published monthly by Industry Publishers, Inc., 1545 N.E. 123rd Street, North Miami, Fla. 33161.

Tennis: Magazine of the Racquet Sports. Published by Golf Digest/Tennis, Inc., 5520 Park Ave., Trumbull, Conn. 06611.

Tennis USA. Official publication of the USTA. A newspaper published 12 times annually by Family Media Inc., 3 Park Ave., New York, N.Y. 10016.

World Tennis. Published monthly by FM Projects, Inc., 3 Park Ave., New York, N.Y. 10016. *World Tennis* is the magazine of membership of the USTA.

Appendix 1   *Tennis Knowledge Test and Answers*

Try the test *before* you read the book. You'll know the answers to some questions just based on your past experience in tennis and in other sports and based on your exposure to tennis through the news media and television. Use a separate piece of paper as an answer sheet; then you'll be able to use the test over and over to assess your improvement in knowledge and understanding. Grade the paper by using the answer key on page 144, and compare your first score with our rating system to see where you stand when you start. *Then* read the book, listen to your instructor, practice the skills, play the game and try the test again. We hope that you'll be pleased with your progress.

For each question that you miss, review the pages referred to in the parentheses beside the question. And write to us if your interpretation differs from ours! Knowledge of these facts and concepts, especially if you can apply them appropriately, will help you to enjoy your participation in tennis both as a spectator and as a player.

The test has been organized into sections to facilitate self-testing as you complete the various chapters.

Unit I contains questions on beginning skills, the forehand and backhand drives, the ready position and basic footwork. It is based on the descriptions in Chapter 2.

Unit II is a quiz of your knowledge of the basic serve and the volley. This material is also found in Chapter 2.

Unit III is based on Chapter 3 and covers more advanced skills, including the lob, the overhead, advanced serves, approaching the net, and the use of spin.

Unit IV is a test of the basic rules, all of which are described in Chapter 6.

Unit V is a test of more advanced rules, including tiebreaker procedures; it is also based on Chapter 6.

Unit VI has to do with general principles of strategy, what shot to use in specific situations and how to attack an opponent's weakness; it is based on Chapter 5.

Unit VII covers the unwritten rules, etiquette and appropriate behavior, all of which are described in Chapter 7.

Unit VIII deals with your general knowledge of the game, including an understanding of equipment, terminology, tournaments, where to play, and governing organizations. This material is provided in Chapters 1, 8, 9, and 10.

Directions: All questions are written for right-handed players. *Read each question carefully.* For multiple choice questions, select the *BEST* answer. For true and false questions, if the statement is true, write a T; if the statement is false or partially false, write an F.

UNIT I: BEGINNING SKILLS

Multiple Choice

1. What is the ready position in which a player should wait for the opponent to return the ball? (pp. 9–10)
   a. The weight well back on the heels and the knees straight.
   b. The weight forward on the balls of the feet, the feet slightly apart and the knees bent.
   c. The weight forward on the balls of the feet, the feet close together and the knees straight.
   d. The feet wide apart, the knees bent and the body turned for a forehand drive.
2. In hitting a backhand drive, what is the most desirable spot to contact the ball? (pp. 19–20)
   a. Opposite the rear foot.
   b. Just ahead of the rear foot.
   c. Opposite the center of the body.
   d. Opposite the forward foot.
   e. Just ahead of the forward foot.
3. In hitting a groundstroke, where should the weight of the player be at the moment of impact? (pp. 14, 20, 22)
   a. On the rear foot.
   b. Evenly distributed on both feet.
   c. On the forward foot.
   d. In front of the forward foot.
4. Which of the following actions should be emphasized more than usual when stroking a low-bouncing ball? (p. 12)
   a. Shorten the backswing.
   b. Shorten the follow-through.
   c. Loop the forward swing.
   d. Bend the knees.
   e. Drop the racket head.
5. What should a player do to insure proper timing? (pp. 25–26, 28)
   a. Start to move into position as the ball bounces.
   b. Start the backswing after moving into position.
   c. Attempt to get in the direct path of the oncoming ball.
   d. Start to move into position as soon as the ball leaves the opponent's racket.

True and False

6. When using the forehand grip, the thumb extends up the top plate of the handle of the racket.   (p. 11)
7. In the forehand grip, the forefinger is extended directly up the handle of the racket.   (p. 11)
8. When the player grips the racket, the racket face should be at right angles to the ground.   (pp. 10–11)
9. In executing a forehand or backhand drive, the follow-through should be in the direction of the intended ball flight.   (pp. 16–17, 20, 22)
10. In hitting a forehand drive, the ball should be contacted when it is opposite the rear foot.   (pp. 15, 22)
11. As part of the preparation for a forehand drive, the player should turn toward the right-hand alley.   (p. 12)
12. A beginner should attempt to play the ball when it is approximately hip high (after the bounce).   (pp. 12, 14)
13. In the backhand grip, the palm of the racket hand should be facing the ground.
                                                                                 (pp. 17–18)
14. In hitting a backhand drive, the player should look over the right shoulder at the oncoming ball.   (p. 19)
15. When hitting a backhand drive, the elbow should lead the racket head through the forward swing.   (p. 20)
16. In executing a backhand drive, the player should use the forehand grip.
                                                                                 (pp. 17–18)
17. In executing a drive, the beginner should stroke the ball on the rise or as soon after the bounce as possible.   (p. 14)
18. In hitting a drive, the beginner should look at the desired target on the other side of the net.   (pp. 15, 20)
19. The same racket face should contact the ball on both the forehand and backhand drives.   (pp. 21–22)
20. In executing a groundstroke, you should swing the racket head forward rapidly (you should hear the "swish") through the point of contact.   (pp. 15, 20)

UNIT II: BASIC SERVE AND VOLLEY

Multiple Choice

1. Which of the following applies to the volley?   (p. 36)
    a. It requires a long, vigorous forward swing.
    b. It is used primarily from the backcourt.
    c. It is used primarily in the forecourt.
    d. It is most frequently hit with a backhand.
2. In hitting a flat volley, where should the ball be contacted?   (pp. 36–38)
    a. In front of the volleyer and below the level of the net.
    b. Behind the volleyer and above the level of the net.
    c. Behind the volleyer and as high as possible.
    d. In front of the volleyer and as high as possible.

3. Which of the following describes correct footwork when hitting a forehand volley?
    (pp. 38, 40)
    a. The player remains in the ready position facing the net and the feet do not move.
    b. The shoulders turn so the left side is toward the net while the left foot steps across the body forward toward the ball.
    c. The right foot steps forward toward the ball, body facing the net.
    d. The right foot steps backward away from the ball, bringing the body into the correct side-to-net position with the left shoulder toward the net.
4. Which of the following coaching cues applies primarily to the volley?   (p. 40)
    a. Swing down together-up together.
    b. Punch the ball.
    c. Hit up and out—over the ball.
    d. Swing from low to high.
    e. Take your racket back early.
5. You are standing in a good net position and your opponent hits a hard drive right at the middle of your body. How should you handle this challenge?   (p. 37)
    a. Use a backhand volley; place the racket face in front of your body directly in the path of the oncoming ball.
    b. Use a forehand volley; place the racket face in front of your body directly in the path of the oncoming ball.
    c. Duck! and stay away from the net when playing this opponent.
    d. Pout! and accuse your opponent of poor behavior for hitting the ball right at you.

True and False

6. The server's left side should point toward the intended direction of the serve.
    (p. 30)
7. In preparing to serve, the balls should be held in the palm of the tossing hand.
    (p. 31)
8. In tossing the ball for the serve, the ball should be released from the tossing hand as the racket begins to swing down.   (p. 32)
9. During the serve backswing, the elbow should be high and the racket head should drop behind the head and practically scratch the back.   (p. 32)
10. The recommended point of contact for the basic flat serve is above and in front of the right shoulder.   (p. 34)
11. When serving, the ball should be hit with the racket arm fully extended.   (p. 34)
12. The server's arm and wrist action should be tense.   (pp. 32–35)
13. During the forward swing of the serve, you should rotate your trunk and shift your weight forward.   (p. 34)
14. When serving, the forward swing should be downward.   (pp. 34–35)
15. The body should "jackknife" forward during the follow-through of the serve.
    (p. 34)

UNIT III: ADVANCED SKILLS

Multiple Choice

1. What is the advantage of imparting topspin to the ball on a groundstroke?   (p. 42)
   a. Imparting topspin allows a player to hit the ball harder since the ball will dip downward in its flight.
   b. The ball will be more stable in its flight and will slow up on its bounce.
   c. A topspin drive will bounce lower than will a ball with either backspin or no spin imparted to it.
   d. There is no advantage whatsoever in imparting topspin to a ball.
2. If other things are equal, a drive hit with which of the following will have the greatest speed?   (pp. 41–43)
   a. Backspin
   b. Topspin
   c. Sidespin
   d. No spin
3. How is underspin applied to a backhand?   (pp. 42–43)
   a. Start with the racket head at a point below ball level, swing up and follow-through high.
   b. Turn your wrist over as you hit.
   c. Start with the racket head at a point above ball level, swing down and follow-through low.
   d. Tilt the racket backward so the face is slightly open to the sky.
4. When serving, why is it desirable to put spin on the ball?   (pp. 43–44)
   a. It causes the ball to bounce in an unexpected manner, thus making it more difficult to return.
   b. It permits greater control of the ball.
   c. It permits a wider margin of error as the ball crosses the net and causes the ball to drop more rapidly within the service court.
   d. All of these.
   e. None of these.
5. In serving an American twist, where should you toss the ball?   (pp. 32, 44)
   a. Directly in front of you.
   b. To your left and slightly behind you.
   c. To your right and slightly behind you.
   d. To your right and slightly in front of you.
6. What factors should be considered by the receiver in planning the target for the return of serve?   (pp. 45, 76–77)
   a. The receiver's capabilities.
   b. The server's stroke weaknesses.
   c. The server's anticipated actions immediately after the serve, e.g., does the server stay back or come up to the net.
   d. Statements a and b above.
   e. All of the above.
7. Which of the following is characteristic of a good approach shot?   (p. 46)
   a. Hit deep to the opponent's backcourt as fast as possible.
   b. Hit deep to opponent's strength.
   c. Hit short to opponent's weakness.
   d. Hit deep with underspin and medium speed.
   e. Hit short with underspin and slow speed to opponent's weakness.

8. When rushing the net, which of the following is most important in making the first volley? (pp. 46–47)
   a. Hit it on the run in order to get into good net position as quickly as possible.
   b. Run forward, stop and get set, volley, then move forward another few steps.
   c. Run forward, stop and get set, then wait to see where your opponent is going to hit.
   d. Wait to see where your opponent hits the ball, then run forward to hit the volley.
9. What is the purpose of the lob? (pp. 47–48)
   a. To gain time in order to return to a ready position.
   b. To force your opponent from the net.
   c. To give the player time to go to the net.
   d. All of the above.
   e. Statements a and b above.
10. When using a lob, generally where is it most advisable to place the ball? (p. 48)
   a. Near the baseline.
   b. Close to the service line.
   c. Just over the opponent's head.
   d. To the opponent's backhand.
   e. Close to the sideline.

True and False

11. In a slice serve, when the face of the racket contacts the ball, the face of the racket is flat, directly behind the ball. (pp. 32, 43)
12. In receiving a serve sliced wide to the right court, the receiver should stay behind the baseline and move laterally to the right. (p. 45)
13. When a server delivers an especially hard flat serve, the receiver should take a longer backswing. (p. 45)
14. In returning a lob with an overhead smash, proper body position is directly behind the intended point of contact. (p. 50)
15. The closer you are to the net, the better your chance of hitting an effective drop shot. (pp. 50–51)

UNIT IV: BASIC RULES

Multiple Choice

1. What choice is given the winner of the toss? (p. 82)
   a. End of the court.
   b. Serving or receiving.
   c. Serving, receiving, or end of the court.
   d. The number of games to be played in each set.
   e. Serve and end, or receiving.
2. What is the decision when the server tosses the ball up and catches it instead of striking at it? (pp. 32, 83)
   a. A fault should be called.
   b. A let should be called.
   c. The server may try again without penalty.
   d. The server may try again, but if the same action is repeated, a fault occurs.

3. Which of the following is a foot fault?   (pp. 82–83)
   a. The server steps over the baseline just before the served ball crosses the net.
   b. The server steps over the baseline before the racket strikes the ball.
   c. The server's feet are both off the ground when the ball is struck.
   d. None of these.
4. The server serves before the receiver is ready and the receiver does not attempt to
   return the serve. What is the decision?   (p. 85)
   a. A fault is called.
   b. A let is called.
   c. A point is awarded to the server.
   d. A point is awarded to the receiver.
5. On the second serve, the server serves underhand into the proper service court, and
   the receiver makes no effort to return it, claiming that the serve was delivered incorrectly. What is the ruling?   (p. 83)
   a. The server wins the point.
   b. The receiver wins the point.
   c. A let is called and the ball is re-served.
   d. The point is re-played.
6. During the serve, where must the receiver stand?   (p. 84)
   a. Anywhere on the receiver's side of the net.
   b. Anywhere, except within the service court.
   c. Anywhere within the court boundaries.
   d. Anywhere outside the court boundaries.
7. A ball is considered out when it hits   (p. 86)
   a. completely behind the line.
   b. just the back edge of the line.
   c. more off than on the line.
   d. any part of the line.
   e. completely in front of the line.
8. In a match between Jane and Karen, there is a long rally. During the rally, Jane
   swings at the ball and misses it; the ball lands outside the baseline. What is the
   ruling?   (pp. 85–86)
   a. Point for Jane.   d. Fault.
   b. Point for Karen.   e. Legal, the ball remains in play.
   c. Let.
9. In which of the following situations does the player **not** lose the point? (pp. 85–86)
   a. The ball bounces twice before the player makes the return.
   b. The player, standing behind the baseline, catches the ball before it bounces.
   c. In singles, the player's return lands in the opponent's alley.
   d. During a rally, the player's return touches the net as it passes over and then lands
      in the opponent's backcourt.
   e. None of these.
10. Which of the following is **not** a good return?   (pp. 85–86)
   a. The ball passes outside the net post and lands in the court.
   b. The player follows through over the net.
   c. The player reaches over the net to play a ball which has bounced back over the
      net before it could be reached.
   d. The player volleys a ball before it passes the net.
   e. All of these.

11. Where should the service be made when the score is 40-love?   (pp. 83, 86)
    a. From the right side of the court.
    b. From the left side of the court.
    c. From either side, depending upon the side from which the game was started.
    d. From either side, depending upon the side from which the last service was made.
12. The score is deuce; the receiver wins the next point. What is the score? (pp. 86–87)
    a. Game for the receiver.   d. Advantage in.
    b. 40–30.   e. Advantage out.
    c. 30–40.
13. Using the traditional scoring system, when is a game completed?   (p. 87)
    a. When one side has won four points and the opponents have not more than two points.
    b. When one side has won four points and the opponents have won three.
    c. When a total of four points has been played.
    d. When either side wins five points.
14. Which of the following scores is a completed set?   (p. 87)
    a. 4–2   d. 6–4
    b. 6–5   e. 5–1
    c. 9–8
15. When should players change ends of the court? When the score is   (p. 87)
    a. 6–0.   c. 5–7, 6–4, 1–3.
    b. 6–3, 3–5.   d. 3–6, 6–1.
16. In doubles, where must the server's partner stand?   (p. 89)
    a. Anywhere in the partner's half of the serving court.
    b. Anywhere on the server's side of the net providing that this position does not obstruct the view of any player.
    c. Anywhere on their side of the net if the position is within the court boundaries.
    d. Anywhere on their side of the net regardless of boundaries or other players.
17. In a doubles game, on the second serve, the server serves the ball which hits the net cord and then drops into the receiver's alley. The receiver cannot reach it in time to return it. What is the ruling?   (p. 84)
    a. The serve is a let.   c. The server wins the point.
    b. The serve is a fault.   d. The server loses the point.
18. In the first game of a men's doubles match, Adam received serve in the right court and his partner, Brent, received serve in the left court. In the second game, when they serve, which partner must serve?   (pp. 89–90)
    a. Since Adam received serve in the right court, he must be his team's first server.
    b. Since Adam was the first receiver, he must be the first server.
    c. Since Brent was the second receiver, he must be the first server.
    d. Since the order of serving and the order of receiving are independent of each other, either partner may serve first.
19. When may a doubles team change its order of serving?   (p. 89)
    a. At the beginning of any game in a set.
    b. At anytime during the match.
    c. At the beginning of any set.
    d. The serving order may not be changed.
20. In doubles, when may the order of receiving be altered?   (p. 89)
    a. At any time during the match.
    b. When the service changes.
    c. When the teams change ends of the court.
    d. When the next set starts.
    e. Never; the receiving order may not be changed.

UNIT V: ADVANCED RULES

Multiple Choice

1. Player A's first serve is a fault. After the second serve, which is good, a dog runs across the court, interfering with the opponent, player B. What is the decision?   (p. 84)
   a. The point is awarded to player B because of the interference.
   b. Play continues.
   c. The second serve must be re-served.
   d. The whole point is re-played and two serves are allowed the server.
2. The score is 15–30. By error, the server serves from the right half of the court and delivers a fault. The error is then discovered. What is the score and where should the server stand to deliver the next serve?   (p. 83)
   a. 15–40, no faults, right court.
   b. 15–30, one fault, right court.
   c. 15–40, one fault, left court.
   d. 15–30, one fault, left court.
3. During a rally, Brent throws his racket at the ball; the ball hits the racket and re-bounds over the net into the court. What is the ruling?   (pp. 85–86)
   a. The point is re-played.   c. Brent's opponent wins the point.
   b. Brent wins the point.   d. The ball continues in play.
4. Tom is serving in a doubles game between Tom and Betty and Bill and Mary. The score is 30–15 and one fault has been served when it is discovered that Betty should have been serving. Which of the following procedures is correct?   (p. 89)
   a. The score remains at 30–15, one fault, and Tom continues serving the rest of the game.
   b. The score remains at 30–15, one fault, and Betty serves the rest of the game.
   c. The score becomes 30 all and Tom continues to serve the rest of the game.
   d. The score becomes 30 all and Betty serves the rest of the game.
   e. None of the above answers are correct. (Describe the correct procedure.)
5. A doubles team changes its order of receiving by mistake and it is not discovered until the score is 15-love. What is the decision?   (p. 90)
   a. Players switch immediately to reestablish the proper order.
   b. Players switch at the beginning of the next game in which they are the receivers to reestablish the proper order.
   c. The reversed order is continued until the end of the set.
   d. The reversed order is continued until the end of the match.
6. What happens if your lob hits one of the overhead lights?   (p. 85)
   a. You play the point over.
   b. You lose the point.
   c. You win the point.
   d. The ball remains in play.
   e. The point is re-played, but you get only one serve.
7. In doubles, the first serve hits the receiver's partner (who is standing on the service line) before it touches the ground. What is the decision?   (pp. 85, 90)
   a. The serve is a fault.   c. The serving team wins the point.
   b. The serve is a let.   d. The receiving team wins the point.
8. How much time do players have when changing ends (from the end of the game to the first serve of the next game)?   (p. 88)
   a. 30 seconds.   c. 90 seconds.
   b. 60 seconds.   d. 2 minutes.

9. Normally, tiebreaker procedures begin when the games are tied at   (p. 90)
   a. 5–5.   c. 7–7.
   b. 6–6.   d. 8–8.
10. In the 12-point tiebreaker, when do players change ends of the court?   (p. 91)
   a. Never.
   b. After the first point is played.
   c. After two points are played.
   d. After four points are played.
   e. After six points are played.
11. When the score of a 12-point tiebreaker is 4 points all, into which court is the ninth
    point served?   (p. 91)
   a. The right court.   c. The court the server chooses.
   b. The left court.   d. The court the receiver chooses.
12. In a mixed doubles match, Joe and Sue are playing Don and Peggy. Joe served the
    first game, Don the second game, Sue the third game and Peggy the fourth game.
    The match is close and finally reaches the stage where the 12-point tiebreaker pro-
    cedures go into effect. Who serves the first point of the tiebreaker?   (pp. 91–92)
   a. Joe.   c. Sue.
   b. Don.   d. Peggy.
13. In a mixed doubles match, Joe and Sue are playing Don and Peggy. Joe served the
    first game, Don the second game, Sue the third game and Peggy the fourth game.
    The match is close and finally reaches the stage where the 12-point tiebreaker pro-
    cedures go into effect. When the score reaches 3–2 in the tiebreaker, who serves the
    next two points?   (pp. 91–92)
   a. Joe.   c. Sue.
   b. Don.   d. Peggy.
14. Which of the following point scores indicates that a 12-point tiebreaker has been
    completed?   (p. 90)
   a. 5–4.   d. 7–7.
   b. 7–6.   e. 7–5.
   c. 6–1.
15. In "no-ad" scoring, when the score is tied at 3 points all, into which court is the
    seventh point served?   (p. 93)
   a. The right court.
   b. The left court.
   c. The court the server chooses.
   d. The court the receiver chooses.

UNIT VI: STRATEGY

Multiple Choice

1. You are playing a match against an unknown opponent; when should you begin to
   develop your strategy?   (p. 67)
   a. During the warm-up.
   b. After the first few games of the match have been played.
   c. During the first set.
   d. After the first set has been completed.

2. Which of the following is **not** good strategy?   (pp. 67–72)
   a. Vary the pace and placement of your shots.
   b. Keep your drives low to the net (within one foot), especially when your opponent is in the backcourt.
   c. Hit crosscourt drives when you're in trouble.
   d. Analyze your opponent's strengths and weaknesses.
   e. Play percentage tennis.

3. What does it mean to play percentage tennis?   (pp. 70–71)
   a. Avoid careless errors.
   b. Be aware of the crucial points.
   c. Utilize appropriate shot selection.
   d. All of these.
   e. None of these.

4. In singles, when you have to hit a second serve, what should you be trying to do?   (p. 75)
   a. Hit a flat serve.
   b. Aim at the deep corners of the service court.
   c. Hit a spin serve aimed at the receiver's weakness.
   d. Concentrate on getting it in—hit it much slower and aim at the middle of the service court.

5. What is the usual position of a good player waiting to receive service?   (pp. 45–46, 76–77)
   a. On the service line.
   b. Near the baseline, inside the singles sideline.
   c. Directly behind the alley.
   d. Outside the alley, a step or two nearer to the net than the baseline.
   e. Inside the court boundaries.

6. What is the most important objective in returning serve?   (p. 76)
   a. Get the ball back.
   b. Hit the ball to the server's backhand.
   c. Hit an aggressive shot.
   d. Avoid hitting a short shot.

7. When playing a baseline game, what should the player's position be?   (p. 9)
   a. Approximately three feet behind the baseline.
   b. Right on the baseline.
   c. Between the baseline and the service line.
   d. Halfway between the baseline and the net.

8. In singles, after each stroke made from the baseline, how should you position yourself?   (pp. 67–68)
   a. On a line directly behind the center mark.
   b. Directly behind the right side of the court when your opponent is hitting a forehand.
   c. Directly behind the left side of the court when your opponent is hitting a backhand.
   d. On a line that bisects the angle of your opponent's possible return.
   e. On a line that bisects the angle of your possible return.

9. You are playing a singles match against an opponent who plays a steady baseline game. Which of the following shots might be most effective in attacking this type of opponent?   (p. 77)
   a. Forehand and backhand drives.
   b. Drop shots followed by lobs.
   c. Half volleys.
   d. Hard serves.
   e. Spin serves.

10. What general guideline should govern your approach to the net during a rally?
(pp. 46–47, 78)
   a. Your approach to the net should be preceded by a forcing shot to your opponent's weakness.
   b. Approach the net following a shot hit from behind your baseline.
   c. Continue your approach without stopping until you reach a good net position.
   d. Your approach should bring you to a final position several feet from the net on the center line.

11. If you are at the net, your opponent will have a good chance to pass you when your shot bounces
(p. 78)
   a. just inside the baseline.
   b. in "no-man's land."
   c. on the service line.

12. In singles, assuming that your opponent is a good net player, which of the following strokes would you use when your opponent is at the net and you are in the backcourt?
(pp. 77–78)
   a. A drop shot hit to either side of the court.
   b. A groundstroke hit directly at the net player's body.
   c. A groundstroke hit to the net player's backhand.
   d. A lob hit to the net player's baseline.

13. In singles, if you hit a forehand down the line to your opponent's backhand and follow your shot to the net, where should you stand to anticipate the return?
(pp. 67–68, 78–79)
   a. On the center service line, halfway between the service line and the net.
   b. Two or three feet to the right of the center service line.
   c. Two or three feet to the left of the center service line.
   d. In the service court, two or three feet from the right alley.
   e. In the service court, two or three feet from the left alley.

14. Which of the following is the most important factor in doubles strategy?   (p. 79)
   a. The ability to approach and hold the net position.
   b. Good smashing ability by both partners.
   c. Good speed by at least one partner.
   d. Skill in lobbing.
   e. Control of the backcourt.

15. In doubles tournament play, which player of a team should serve first?   (p. 89)
   a. The player who receives serve in the right court.
   b. The player who receives serve in the left court.
   c. The weaker server.
   d. The stronger server.

16. In doubles, when one partner is serving, what is the correct net position for the other partner?
(pp. 73–74)
   a. One foot from the net.
   b. Three to five feet from the net.
   c. Six to nine feet from the net.
   d. Ten to twelve feet from the net.
   e. On the service line.

17. Which of the following shots is good for returning serve in doubles?
(pp. 44–45, 76–77)
   a. A short lob to the net player.
   b. A high crosscourt floater.
   c. A chip hit crosscourt at the server's feet.
   d. A drop shot.

18. If you have been poaching at net and suddenly your opponent has passed you down your alley, what should your plan be? (p. 107)
    a. Guard the alley thereafter.
    b. Feint as though you were going to poach, hoping to lure the opponent into trying another alley shot.
    c. Continue poaching, figuring it was a lucky shot.
    d. Retreat from the net position and play beside your partner in the backcourt.
19. You and your partner are both in a good net position and your opponents are in the backcourt. One of the opponents sends up a lob that catches you by surprise and your partner runs behind you to cover the lob with an overhead smash. What should you do? (pp. 79–80)
    a. Crouch down below net level.
    b. Quickly run to the other side of the court.
    c. Nothing.
    d. Retreat to the baseline.
20. In doubles, a deep lob return is made by the opponents over the heads of the players at the net. What is the best strategy for the team at the net? (pp. 79–80)
    a. The fastest player should return to the baseline.
    b. The server should return to the baseline.
    c. The receiver should return to the baseline.
    d. The player to whose side of the court the ball has been hit should return to the baseline.
    e. Both partners should return to the baseline.

UNIT VII: ETIQUETTE

Multiple Choice

1. Which of the following is an example of courtesy in tennis? (pp. 97–99)
    a. Calling a let when a ball from another court rolls onto your court during a point.
    b. Calling all balls that hit the line "out"—to give your opponent the benefit of the doubt.
    c. Rolling balls from nearby courts back onto the court from which they came as quickly as possible, even though those players are engaged in playing a point.
    d. When you leave the courts, walking behind players who are still playing points.
2. You are the receiver in the second game of a singles match. The server wants to warm up her serve and insists that it is only common courtesy to permit her all the practice serves she desires. What should you do? (pp. 88–89)
    a. Insist that since play is continuous, she must serve with no practice serves at all.
    b. Agree to play "the first one in."
    c. Allow a mulligan (a third try) if the first two serves are faults.
    d. The unwritten rules support the server's contention and you should permit her all the practice serves that she desires.
3. What should you do if you are unable to determine whether your opponent's shot is good or just out? (p. 97)
    a. Call it out.
    b. Return the ball and if your shot is out, ask to replay the point.
    c. Play the shot as good.
    d. Ask your opponent to make the decision.
    e. Ask a spectator to make the call.

4. You hit a shot into your opponent's court; your opponent is uncertain of the call, but you are positive that your shot was good. What should you do?   (p. 97)
   a. Say "My shot was good!"
   b. Ask to replay the point.
   c. If you are asked how it was, say it was good.
   d. Say "I think the ball was good, but you should call it the way you saw it."
5. What is the best procedure when one of your balls rolls onto a neighboring court where play is in progress?   (p. 97)
   a. Call to a player on that court to return the ball.
   b. Run onto the court and get it out of the way quickly.
   c. Wait until the point is finished on the neighboring court and then ask for it.
   d. Consider it a lost ball which should not be recovered at all.
6. If the opponents lob to your partner who has a very bad overhead, what should you do?   (pp. 98–99)
   a. Encourage him by calling out "Hit it!"
   b. Groan loudly "Oh no, not again!"
   c. Tell him to bounce it and hit the shot as a groundstroke.
   d. Push him out of the way and holler "Mine!"
   e. Say nothing.
7. Toward the end of a long, tough match played under extreme heat, which of the following can you do if you are thoroughly exhausted?   (p. 88)
   a. Request a 5-minute intermission.
   b. Take 90 seconds on each odd game changeover to refresh yourself.
   c. Leave the court area, as long as it is for less than 3 minutes, to get water and/or salt pills.
   d. Ask your opponent to agree to a specified rest period, knowing that the match must continue if no agreement is reached.

True and False

8. The server should announce the score periodically before serving and should always call the server's score first.   (pp. 87, 96)
9. It is considered good tennis etiquette to refrain from poaching.   (pp. 98–99, 107)
10. When you are competing in a tournament as an individual, it is appropriate to accept coaching from your friends when changing ends of the court.   (p. 98)
11. It is considered good tennis etiquette to practice with players of lesser skill occasionally.   (pp. 99–100)
12. Whenever your opponents hit a shot into your court and close to a line, you should call "Good!" to let them know it was in.   (p. 97)
13. Even though your opponent is playing badly, you should not offer your expert advice.   (p. 99)
14. When line umpires are officiating a match, players are supposed to help in calling the lines.   (p. 100)
15. Spectators should applaud good shots as they occur during the rally.   (p. 101)

VIII: GENERAL KNOWLEDGE

Multiple Choice

1. When a team plays every other team in the tournament, what type of tournament is being played?   (pp. 107, 108, 121–123)
   a. Single elimination.
   b. Double elimination.
   c. Ladder.
   d. Round robin.
   e. Consolation.
2. Which of the following gives correct information concerning stringing?
   (pp. 113–114)
   a. Nylon is affected by changes in temperature.
   b. Nylon is comparatively expensive.
   c. Gut is affected by moisture.
   d. Gut has comparatively little elasticity.
   e. Gut is more durable but less resilient than nylon.
3. Which of the following organizations governs the play of tennis in this country?
   (pp. 115–117)
   a. United States Tennis Association.
   b. United States Lawn Tennis Association.
   c. American Tennis Association.
   d. Association of Tennis Professionals.
   e. National Public Parks Tennis Association.
4. What does it mean when the TV announcer says, "It's match point!"?   (p. 106)
   a. The next point could complete the match.
   b. If the server wins the next point, the server wins the match.
   c. In the deciding set of the match, the score at that particular point is tied in the number of games won.
   d. The receiver can make a service break by winning the next point.
5. What is meant by the term "not up"?   (p. 106)
   a. The player's racket hit the ground before it hit the ball.
   b. The player missed the ball completely.
   c. The ball bounced twice before the player hit it.
   d. The ball hit the net before the player hit it.
   e. The ball landed outside the court boundaries.
6. If your opponent lobs you, what is your return called?   (p. 106)
   a. Overhand.   d. Overhand or overhead.
   b. Overhead.   e. Overhead or smash.
   c. Smash.
7. What is the meaning of the term "ace"?   (p. 102)
   a. The server won the point.
   b. The first serve was a good serve.
   c. The receiver was unable to return a good service.
   d. The receiver was unable to reach a good service.
8. Who competes in Davis Cup matches?   (p. 103)
   a. Men of all countries.
   b. Women of all countries.
   c. Men and women of England and the United States.
   d. Women of England and the United States.
   e. Men and women of the United States only.

9. What term refers to a point that must be re-played?   (p. 106)
   a. Net ball.   d. Deuce.
   b. Let.   e. Dead ball.
   c. Fault.
10. Where is "no-man's land"?   (p. 106)
   a. In the alley on either side of the court.
   b. The forecourt area near the net.
   c. The midcourt area, behind the service line.
   d. The backcourt area near the baseline.
   e. Behind the baseline.
11. What is it called when a ball is returned immediately after its bounce?   (p. 105)
   a. A volley.   d. A courtesy stroke.
   b. A drop volley.   e. A groundstroke.
   c. A half volley.
12. When a player receives a "bye" in a tournament, the player is   (p. 102)
   a. placed against an easy opponent.
   b. eliminated from the tournament.
   c. advanced to the next round of the tournament.
   d. privileged to select a desirable first round opponent.
13. How can you be certain that the tennis balls you purchase meet official specifications?   (pp. 114–115)
   a. Buy pressureless balls.
   b. Buy those labeled "USTA approved."
   c. Buy those labeled "For Championship Play."
   d. Buy heavy-duty white balls.
   e. Buy those endorsed by the WITA.
14. Winning the Grand Slam is a prized goal of the world's highly-ranked players. Which nations' championships are included in the Grand Slam?   (p. 105)
   a. Australia, England, France, United States.
   b. Australia, England, Italy, United States.
   c. England (Wimbledon) and the United States.
   d. Australia, England, and United States.
   e. England, France, Italy, United States.
15. Which of the following services are provided by the USTA and the sectional associations?   (pp. 115–117)
   a. Sanctioning and scheduling of tournaments.
   b. Rankings of players in more than 50 categories.
   c. Certification of tennis teachers.
   d. Insurance programs for members.
   e. Choices a and b above.

KNOWLEDGE TEST ANSWER KEY

Unit I: Beginning Skills

1. b	6. F	11. T	16. F
2. e	7. F	12. T	17. F
3. c	8. T	13. T	18. F
4. d	9. T	14. T	19. F
5. d	10. F	15. F	20. T

Unit V: Advanced Rules

1. d	6. b	11. a
2. d	7. c	12. e
3. c	8. c	13. d
4. b	9. b	14. e
5. b	10. e	15. d

Unit II: Basic Serve and Volley

1. c	6. T	11. T
2. d	7. F	12. F
3. b	8. F	13. T
4. b	9. T	14. F
5. a	10. T	15. F

Unit VI: Strategy

1. a	6. a	11. c	16. d
2. b	7. a	12. d	17. c
3. d	8. d	13. b	18. b
4. c	9. b	14. a	19. b
5. b	10. a	15. d	20. e

Unit III: Advanced Skills

1. a	6. e	11. F
2. d	7. d	12. F
3. c	8. b	13. F
4. d	9. d	14. F
5. b	10. a	15. T

Unit VII: Etiquette

1. a	6. e	11. T
2. a	7. b	12. F
3. c	8. T	13. T
4. d	9. F	14. F
5. c	10. F	15. F

Unit IV: Basic Rules

1. c	6. a	11. b	16. d
2. c	7. a	12. e	17. d
3. b	8. a	13. a	18. d
4. b	9. d	14. d	19. c
5. a	10. d	15. d	20. d

Unit VIII: General Knowledge

1. d	6. e.	11. c
2. c	7. d	12. c
3. a	8. a	13. b
4. a	9. b	14. a
5. c	10. c	15. e

RATING SYSTEM (135 possible)

120 or better:	Smashing! You could be a pro!
105–119:	Well done! You're doing all right.
95–104:	Pretty good—might check out the ones you missed.
80–94:	You must have lost your grip—better read the book (again)!!
79 or less:	Start now, hit the book and get on the ball.

ANSWERS TO EVALUATION QUESTIONS

Page	*Answer and Page Reference*
20	If you contact the ball earlier, your opponent will have less time to prepare. (p. 14)
22	Performance question.
22	Performance question.
25	Use of the two-handed backhand results in a strong swing, compensates for weak wrists and arms, and facilitates the application of topspin. On the negative side, it shortens the reach, makes the application of slice and backspin difficult, poses a problem in returning high bouncing balls, and requires quicker responses. (p. 23)
34	Performance question.
37	In the ready position for volleying, the racket head is held at approximately eye level. In volleying a slow moving ball, the backswing may need to be lengthened to add power to the stroke. (pp. 36–40)
40	Performance question.
44	Backspin is used to hit drop shots; topspin is used to keep your opponent deep. A right-to-left sidespin will cause the ball to bounce toward the opponent's left sideline. (pp. 41–43, 50)
46	Try to slice high bouncing topspin serves from within the baseline. (pp. 43, 45)
51	Performance question.
54	Performance question.
55	Performance question.
55	Performance question.
67	Performance question.
71	To the right. (pp. 67–68)
72	To gain a psychological edge, try to win the first point in each game, and the first game in the set; be prepared to go all out immediately as the match starts; anticipate so that you can easily play balls your opponent thought were sure winners; and maintain your calm on critical points and games. (pp. 66–72)
75	C–D. Players are side by side in good net position from which they should be able to control the net. Probably the best attack against such a strong position is to lob over their heads, attempting to force them into the backcourt. A–B is a very weak position, subject to attack down either sideline or diagonally between the players. While maintaining parallel position, E and F are too far from the net to hit aggressive volleys and are subject to attack by low shots hit to their feet. (pp. 73–74)
76	In the right service court, No. 2 or No.4, and in the left court, No. 7 or No. 9. The choice depends on your opponent; try to force a return from the opponent's weakest stroke. Occasionally serve directly at your opponent, No. 3 and No. 8. A slice serve to No. 1 forces the receiver out of position most. By serving to No. 4 or No. 7, the server has automatically "bisected the angle." (pp. 44, 67–68, 75–76)

87   The score is love–15; 30–love; 40–15; 40–30; 15 all; deuce; advantage server; deuce; advantage receiver; game receiver. (pp. 86–87)

88   No maximum time between points is specified, although the receiver must play to the reasonable pace of the server; 90 seconds are allowed for changing ends.   (pp. 85, 88)

93   At 6 games all, one tiebreaker game concludes the set, thus avoiding what could become a very long advantage set. The 12 point tiebreaker requires one player to be ahead by 2 points, so the "sudden death" point (when either player can win the match by winning that point) never occurs.   (pp. 90, 93)

96   Answers follow the quiz.   (pp. 94–101)

115   Younger and less strong players appreciate a lighter weight racket. Baseline players tend to prefer head-heavy rackets. Racket flexibility dampens vibration and helps absorb shock.   (pp. 111–113)

118   Do not distract the players in any way: applaud only the good shots; do not talk loudly, do not coach either player, do not "help" with line calls. Observe from various view points; look at strokes and strategies; analyze strengths and weaknesses of both players.
          (p. 101)

Appendix 2   Do You Know the Score?

This self-testing quiz was developed for use in a competitive mixed doubles league, and is presented here for your thoughtful participation. Underlying concepts are discussed in Chapter 7: The Unwritten Rules. Additional insights may be obtained by reading "The Code," a USTA publication included in the Selected References list. Answers may be found on page 149.

Directions: On a separate piece of paper, write the numbers of *all the appropriate choices* for each question. Some questions have more than one correct answer. Justify each choice in one or two sentences. If you think there is an answer better than any of those listed, *describe* and *justify* your answer.

1. Your partner is having a miserable day—almost every shot is just out, goes right to the opposing net player, or just catches the tape. What should you do?
   a. Complain to your partner; tell him/her to get with it.
   b. Mumble under your breath, but smile sweetly.
   c. Play your best—concentrate on each shot.
   d. Make excuses to your opponents by saying, "It's obvious we'd win except my partner is playing so terribly!"
   e. Quit, since obviously your team doesn't have a chance.
   f. Encourage your partner, without making your partner feel self-conscious; be supportive, calm.
2. You and your partner disagree about whether your opponent's shot was in or out. What should your team do?
   a. Since the call is questionable, play the point over.
   b. Call the ball out and take the point.
   c. Call the ball good and give your opponents the point.
   d. Ask your friends sitting in the bleachers to make the call.
   e. Stand there and argue.
3. Your opponents are just plain unpleasant. They scowl at you, refuse to hit the ball to you during the warm-up, behave in a superior manner, etc. What can you do?
   a. Ignore them—say nothing; stay behind an icy curtain.
   b. Retaliate by scowling back and behaving unpleasantly yourself.
   c. Be polite, smile pleasantly and concentrate on hitting your shots.

4. You and your partner are obviously better and more experienced players than your opponents. What kind of behavior should you demonstrate?
    a. Be condescending—after all, why should they waste your time?
    b. Goof off—since you know you'll win anyway; try all your cute shots. Be sure to giggle a lot!
    c. Be a show-off (hot dog!). You're better and everyone knows it, so blast away with more than full power.
    d. Be polite and encouraging—play your best shots; be pleasant when they make a good effort.
    e. Super sweet—encourage them on every shot even if it was a poor effort.
5. Suppose you and your partner are obviously the weaker players. How would you like to see your opponents behave? Use one of the choices in the previous question.
6. You and your partner are obviously weaker and less experienced than your opponents. What kind of behavior should you demonstrate?
    a. Give up—obviously you'll lose, so why try?
    b. Sarcastic—especially when they miss one of their hot dog shots.
    c. Play your best, win as many points as you can and admire their good shots.
    d. Act embarrassed and apologetic for not giving them better competition.
7. Suppose you and your partner are obviously the stronger players. How would you like to see your opponents behave? Use one of the choices in the previous question.
8. Your team seems to be playing pretty well and your skills are not obviously less than your opponents, but you're losing. What can you do to turn the tide of the match?
    a. Concentrate—focus on each shot.
    b. Perform the fundamentals: watch the ball, get into good position for each shot, hit through the ball, recover position immediately.
    c. Distract them: have an argument about a line call, tell the guy what a great overhead he's got, tell the girl she hits a mean volley, notice the birds, the cars, the people, the feather on the court, the kites in the air, whatever.
    d. Play high percentage shots, i.e, when receiving serve, return crosscourt or lob—don't chance the riskier down-the-line shot.
    e. Analyze their weaknesses and exploit them—if the girl is the weaker player, hit to her whenever you have a chance; if the guy poaches too much, hit behind him or lob over his head; if either player has a weak second serve, move in a step or two to receive it.
    f. Cheat—call the lines a little closer, always in your favor, of course.
9. You've been getting some bad calls in a close match. What should you do?
    a. Tell your opponents that they are cheating.
    b. Give your opponents some bad calls in return.
    c. After the second or third bad call, ask opponents if they are sure of the call.
    d. If you are *sure* they are cheating, ask for help from match officials.
    e. Ask your friends to heckle.
10. You and your partner are both off your game. What should you do?
    a. Clown around a lot, so that if you lose, it doesn't matter since you didn't really try.
    b. Practice your form—at least have a good-looking game.
    c. Worry about the shots you can't seem to hit and keep trying them, even if they don't work.
    d. Play the best you can with whatever shots are working.
    e. Cry and scream and throw a tantrum—swear, stamp your feet, and solicit aid from heaven!
11. Is there some general principle, some thread, that ties these situations and the appropriate responses together? Answer in one or two sentences.

ANSWERS TO "DO YOU KNOW THE SCORE?"

Comments are those made by students who participated in the competitive mixed doubles league.

1. Choices c and f. Don't let your partner get you down; if you play well, you take pressure off your partner who may then relax and play better. Read *Snoopy's Tennis Book*.
2. Choice c. The benefit of the doubt goes to your opponents; if you don't see it out, you call it good.
3. Choice c. If you retaliate in kind, you just sacrifice your own integrity and self-respect. It is possible they are just uptight about the match; they may relax and be more human as the match progresses.
4. Choice d. Respect the dignity of their effort.
5. Choice d. There is no one who at some time or other has not been the weaker player. I don't want to win points because people give them to me; you really haven't won anything when that happens.
6. Choice c. Play with dignity.
7. Choice c. It's no challenge at all to play against quitters.
8. Choices a, b, d and e.
9. Choices c and d.
10. Although I've tried them all (!), choice d has been the most effective. Flexibility and determination can often turn a match around.
11. Never make fun of others; treat them as you would like to be treated. "Do unto others. . . . " *YOU,* and only you, are responsible for your behavior; regardless of the situation, you should behave in a manner consistent with your standards. Be loyal and supportive of your partner. Play your best, no matter what is going on around you; having a courteous, respectful attitude creates the kind of atmosphere which facilitates everyone's best effort. Know the rules, know your rights and deal with situations on the basis of sound knowledge and courtesy. Courtesy and competitive spirit can exist simultaneously.

Appendix 3 USTA and USTA Section Addresses

USTA Inc.
1212 Avenue of the Americas
New York, New York 10036

USTA Center for Education
and Recreational Tennis
729 Alexander Road
Princeton, New Jersey 08540

Caribbean Tennis Association
P.O. Box 40456
Minillas Station
Santurce, Puerto Rico 00940

Eastern Tennis Association
202 Mamaroneck Avenue
White Plains, New York 10601

Florida Tennis Association
9620 Northeast 2nd Avenue
Room 209
Miami Shores, Florida 33138

Hawaii-Pacific Tennis Association
P. O. Box 411
Honolulu, Hawaii 96809

Intermountain Tennis Association
1201 South Parker Road
Room 102
Denver, Colorado 80231

Mid-Atlantic Tennis Association
P.O. Drawer F
Springfield, Virginia 22151

Middle States Tennis Association
939 Radnor Road
Wayne, Pennsylvania 19087

Missouri Valley Tennis Association
722 Walnut
Suite 1
Kansas City, Missouri 64106

New England Lawn Tennis Association
P.O. Box 223
Needham, Massachusetts 02192

Northern California Tennis Association
645 5th Street
San Francisco, California 94107

Northwestern Tennis Association
5525 Cedar Lake Road
St. Louis Park, Minnesota 55416

Pacific Northwest Tennis Association
01875 S. W. Palatine Hill Road
Portland, Oregon 97219

Southern California Tennis Association
Los Angeles Tennis Center
P.O. Box 240015
Los Angeles, California 90024

Southern Tennis Association
3121 Maple Drive, N.E.
Room 29
Atlanta, Georgia 30305

Southwestern Tennis Association
3021 East Farmdale Avenue
Mesa, Arizona 85206

Texas Tennis Association
P.O. Box 192
Austin, Texas 78767

Western Tennis Association
2215 Olympic Street
Springfield, Ohio 45503

Index